Comparative Ethics Series/
Collection d'Éthique Comparée: 1

D1520742

Comparative Ethics Series/
Collection d'Éthique Comparée

As Religious Studies in its various branches has spread out in recent years, it has met with a newly emergent discipline: Comparative Ethics as the study of moralities as cultural systems, rather than as the philosophical investigation of particular moral issues. To study a morality as a dynamic whole in its social nature and functioning requires a context in which other instances of a comparable kind are considered. Moral action-guides and religious action-guides have historically been brought together in mixed, moral-religious or religious-moral systems. The different paths followed by moralities as cultural systems in the varying contexts demand comparative study.

The series embraces three kinds of studies: (1) methodological studies, which will endeavour to elaborate and discuss principles, concepts, and models for the new discipline; (2) studies which aim at deepening our knowledge of the nature and functioning, the scope and content of particular moral systems, such as the Islamic, the Hindu, the Christian, and so on; (3) studies of a directly comparative kind, which bring differing moral systems or elements of systems into relationship.

COMPARATIVE ETHICS

Volume 1

Muslim Ethics and Modernity
A Comparative Study of the Ethical Thought of Sayyid Ahmad Khan and Mawlana Mawdudi

Sheila McDonough

Published for the Canadian Corporation for Studies in Religion/Corporation Canadienne des Sciences Religieuses by Wilfrid Laurier University Press

1984

Canadian Cataloguing in Publication Data

McDonough, Sheila.
  Muslim ethics and modernity

(Comparative ethics series)
Includes bibliographical references and index.
ISBN 0-88920-162-5

1. Maudoodi, Syed Abul 'Ala, Maulana, 1903-
– Ethics. 2. Ahmad Khan, Syed, Sir, 1817-1898 –
Ethics. 3. Islamic ethics. I. Title. II. Series.

BJ1291.M23 1984   297'.5   C84-099634-9

© 1984 Canadian Corporation for Studies in Religion/
    Corporation Canadienne des Sciences Religieuses

84 85 86 87 4 3 2 1

Cover design by Michael Baldwin, MSIAD

Order from:
Wilfrid Laurier University Press
Wilfrid Laurier University
Waterloo, Ontario, Canada   N2L 3C5

ACKNOWLEDGEMENT

This book has been published with the help of a grant from the Canadian Federation for the Humanities, using funds provided by the Social Sciences and Humanities Research Council of Canada.

Table of Contents

Introduction

As systems for communicating, moralities are languages of
persuasion. They seek to convince persons to act in
expected or desired manner by utilizing standardized
vocabularies and rhetoric to invoke particular given
agreements....Such language may appeal either or both to
reason and emotions but in all cases it will be evaluative,
judging behavior as approximating or deviating from
prescribed and proscribed ways of acting. The purpose of
this rhetoric and evaluations is to communicate
expectations and claims in persuasive ways.[1]

My intention is to try to make more intelligible,
especially for non-Muslims, the ethical issues that are
debated among modern Muslims. I hope to do this as a
contribution to Comparative Religious Ethics. I do not
intend to compare Muslim ethics to the ethics of other
traditions, but I do aim to cast the discussion of Muslim
thought into the context of modernity. My method will be
to consider in considerable detail the thinking on ethical
questions of two modern Muslims who have exercised
significant influence on their coreligionists.

The two Muslims in question are Sayyid Ahmad Khan and
Mawlana Mawdudi. Each of these men was motivated by a
strong urge to communicate to his fellow Muslims some new
ethical imperatives. Each has been extremely persuasive.
In both cases the writings and activities have been very
influential in shaping Muslim thought and emotion. Each
has communicated effectively his strong emotions with
respect to the needs of his community. In part, each has
been persuasive because he felt strongly, thought clearly,
and wrote extremely well.

I hope that readers unfamiliar with Islam might gain
from the description of the ethical stances of these two
Muslims some awareness of what it means to be a Muslim
wrestling seriously with the promises and threats of severe
social change. But it should also be remembered that these
are just two of many possible Muslim ethical stances. Both
these men were Sunni Muslims; the Shiah position is

therefore not represented. Both were products of the
Islamic culture of the Indo-Pakistan subcontinent, a
culture different in many respects from other parts of the
Islamic world. India is one country in which Muslims have
always been a minority, although they have often wielded
political power and authority.

Neither of these men represents any classical, or
other Western, or Muslim school of thought. Each is a very
original thinker. Both are trying to use the cumulative
tradition of Islamic ethical thinking, but each selects
from the vast storehouse of that tradition whatever
exemplars, modes of reasoning, ways of interpreting
scripture, and so forth that seem, in his judgment, most
appropriate.[2] Hence, the rhetoric used does appear
persuasive to Muslims because the traditional materials
are used. I shall try to shed some light on how these
traditional materials have been used in putting forward
new ethical perspectives.

I describe Sayyid Ahmad Khan as a rationalist and
Mawlana Mawdudi as a fundamentalist. Sayyid Ahmad Khan has
also often been called a liberal, a modernist, or an
acculturationist. Mawlana Mawdudi has recently been
termed a neofundamentalist, or a neonormativist.[3] I
characterize Sayyid Ahmad Khan as a rationalist because I
think that he was urgently concerned to convince his fellow
Muslims that they must use reason in new ways as a basis
for their individual and collective lives. In other words,
he thought of himself in certain respects as a rationalist.
On the other hand, I do not intend to say that his position
resembles exactly that of any Western, or Muslim school of
thought. He was an original thinker and a serious
religious person. Reason and revelation were not in
conflict in his way of understanding Islam.

In contrast, I describe Mawlana Mawdudi as a
fundamentalist; this term is the nearest approximation I
can find for his position. It might be more illuminating,
and perhaps less pejorative, to use a term such as
neonormativist. I think, however, that there are certain
similarities among fundamentalists as twentieth-century

persons in all religious traditions; for this reason I use
the term. It is true, of course, that Mawdudi's position
has many similarities to that of the nineteenth-century
reformers and iconoclasts who preceded him. But, in my
view, he is more of an ideological thinker than the
earlier reformers were: he aims to put forward a
comprehensive system.

     In these two cases, the rhetoric used does more than
simply invoke agreement about conduct. It is rather a case
of new wine in old bottles. The Muslim community of the
Indo-Pakistan subcontinent has endured a number of severe
shocks--beginning with the failure of the Indian Revolt of
1857, through the partition of the subcontinent in 1947,
until the present. Both thinkers have been acutely aware
of crisis, and have attempted to alleviate the shock and
strain by speaking and writing about new directions that
might be taken. Both believed that ethical thinking was
the most constructive way to guide the members of their
community out of the confusion and despair of their
situation. The aim of the rhetoric, therefore, is not
merely to invoke former agreements, but also to help to
create a new consensus about how Muslims should order
their individual and collective lives.

     Each of these two men is a distinctively modern
person; each stands on the modern side of the chasm of
discontinuity that exists between the medieval world of
life and thought and the realm of modernity. This
discontinuity is a result of changes brought about by the
introduction of technology. Technology brings with it
inevitable transformations in the consciousness of
individuals as they learn new techniques and become more
autonomous individuals. People learn to control machines,
to change their environment, and to become self-reliant.
A modern person tends to distrust traditional authority and
to question readily. He or she has learned that much can
be done to alter conditions of life. Once an individual
experiences the power to change, he or she is much less
likely to accept values without question. This results in
a new need for the individual to be convinced of the

usefulness even of traditional values.

Neither of these men believed that modernity meant the
end of Islam. Each thinks that he has found a way to
transcend the chasm of discontinuity and to relate to the
present and the emerging future in a way that will be
faithful to God. Sayyid Ahmad Khan and Mawdudi each went
through periods of personal searching, and emerged with
visions of Islam which they spent the rest of their lives
trying to communicate. The moralities in each case emerge
out of this synthesising process by which each individual
created what he found to be a reliable way to think and to
act. Each of these Muslims thus became an exemplar in the
realm of ethical thought.

Since each of these men in concerned to persuade
other Muslims to his personal vision of "how to" be
effective as Muslims in the context of modernity, he
necessarily uses the traditional vocabulary and rhetoric.
We will discuss how it happens that these two Muslims,
each using traditional vocabulary, yet arrive at differing
conclusions as to how Muslims should think and act in the
modern world. I am not concerned to argue that either of
these positions represents in any particular sense an
"orthodox" Muslim perspective. Both stances are, I think,
novel, and hence discontinuous with the past. Both have
been, and continue to be persuasive to many well-educated
Muslims. Hence both positions represent possible
interpretations of the Islamic tradition. Many other
interpretations are also possible. I am focussing on
these two because each has been particularly persuasive
as an attempt to put forward Islamic values in the context
of modernity. But I do not wish to imply that either
position is, in any sense, the last word.

I am using the expression "ethical thinking" as a
translation for the Arabic word akhlaq. Recently,
controversy has arisen among persons interested in
comparative religious ethics about how to do comparative
studies of ethics in different societies.[4] We cannot
easily or lightly impose the terms and concepts from one
culture on another; in particular, we need to recognize

that the distinction between ethics and morals is peculiar
to the European languages. The existence of these two
terms derives from our European linguistic origins: one
term comes from Greek, the other from Latin. The
distinction has continued in European languages because of
a habit of making a distinction between what is commonly
felt and done as opposed to what theoretically inclined
thinkers argue is rational or appropriate.[5]

Non-European languages more usually have one word
encompassing morals and ethics, dharma in the Indian case,
for instance, or li in the Chinese. These terms take on,
as we would expect, differing connotations as thought and
practice of the persons using them vary and change
throughout the centuries. Akhlaq is the appropriate term
in Arabic and in the other Islamic languages, such as Urdu,
the language of the two authors we deal with here. The
root from which it derives means to create, to shape, to
give form. Akhlaq is a plural (of khulq) referring to a
collection of distinct traits of character. The knowledge
of morality (ilm-ul-akhlaq) is translated as ethics, moral
sciences. (The dictionary points out that the vice-squad
is the department of akhlaq.[6]) The science of akhlaq was
understood to be a discussion of the way to maintain the
virtues in their optimum state.

My thesis is that each of these modern Muslim ethical
thinkers is aware of a discontinuity between the life and
thought of Muslims in the pre-modern period and the life
of the community in his lifetime. (In Indian Islam, the
break becomes most obvious with the failure of the revolt
of 1857.) Each of these men thus feels strongly that
Muslims cannot simply repeat the habitual patterns of life
and thought of their ancestors. People will have to think
new thoughts and behave in new ways. Yet, as ethical
thinkers, the two Muslims in question wish to affirm that
the ideal of behaviour which they advocate is essentially
faithful to the most basic wisdom of the community. The
original truths that established the community are called
up to legitimate apparent change; change claims in essence
to be a return to fundamental values. The rhetoric used
thus attempts to invoke not the agreement of the immediate

past, but of the far distant and original past that is
thought to be the basic source of the community's life.

The rhetoric does not call up examples only from the
first centry of Islam however. Any facet of the vast
cumulative tradition of Islamic ethical thinking that
seems useful is drawn upon. Each of these two ethical
thinkers was largely self-educated. Each read widely on
his own from the storehouse of the cumulative tradition,
picking up whatever his own reason and intuition told him
might be useful exemplars, modes of reasoning, and
affirmations from the past. To use the cumulative
tradition in this way is not merely to select whatever
pieces from it one might want to use for the new system
one is creating; it also means a change in the way the
whole tradition is to be understood. Each of our two
ethical thinkers is creating his own version of the Islamic
past.

I cannot attempt here to describe the entire
cumulative tradition of Muslim ethical thinking that lies
behind these two men. A comprehensive study of Muslim
ethics has yet to be written. One important recent source,
the manuscript of Abd al-Jabbar, was discovered as recently
as 1951.[7] There may well be other materials yet to be
found that will change the picture we now have of the
development of medieval thought. My own understanding of
the ethical tradition would be similar to that contained
within Marshall Hodgson's three-volume history of the
Islamic peoples, The Venture of Islam: Conscience and
History in a World Civilization.[8] Hodgson's thesis is that
the Muslim conscience expresses itself differently in
different phases of history as Muslims venture to respond
to their understanding of God's purposes for humanity. The
conscience necessarily operates within the limits and
possibilities imposed by the specific situations.

Given the changes brought about by modernity, what
ethical imperatives are most urgent for Muslims? These are
the questions addressed by our two Muslim thinkers. Each
assumes that the Qur'an is the first source for Muslim
values for the issue of reinterpreting the Qur'an has been

central for many modern Muslim thinkers.[9] Mawdudi wrote a
comprehensive commentary on the Qur'an; Sayyid Ahmad Khan
did not do that, but he devoted a great deal of attention
to the Qur'an as the basic source.

The style of the Qur'an tends to be that of speech
directed to an individual listener. The message is that of
a proclamation, a warning that those who hear and
understand should take action immediately to direct
themselves to God. They should cast off disbelief and
scepticism. A Muslim, male or female, is a person who has
responded to the Qur'anic imperative to "believe and do
right." The Qur'an proclaims that right action and right
faith are inextricably linked, yet the final evaluation of
any individual's faith and action will occur only at the
Day of Judgment. Within the context of life on earth, no
individuals have final power to judge other individuals.
There are no priests in Islam, or mediators of God's will
or judgment. Each Muslim alone has to decide for himself
or herself and take the consequences. At any given point
in Muslim history, the majority may and often do hold
certain convictions about appropriate behavior. In
principle, however, since no judgments are final until the
end, God's judgment cannot be mediated within history. Put
simply, any individual Muslim wishing to respond
appropriately to his or her awareness of God's mercy and
goodness may take any amount of help and guidance from
other Muslims and the Islamic past. He or she cannot,
however, find anywhere a guarantee that a given course of
action will inevitably be accepted by God as the right one.
A believer fears God's justice, hopes for God's mercy, and
acts as best he or she can. But until the end, any
evaluation of the appropriateness of given responses is
tentative, and may well be overthrown or reversed.[10]

Because of the uncertainty one cannot really speak of
any interpreters of Islamic ethical thought who might be
considered to have final authority. As indicated above,
the final evaluation rests with God alone. Further, within
history, human arrangements such as the design of the
social order and religious law are human constructs based

on the consensus of the believers. Fazlur Rahman has
indicated in his recent book Major Themes of the Qur'an
that the basic imperative of the Qur'an is that the
individual should cultivate his or her own conscience,
taqwa.[11] The strengthening of consciences allows
individuals to discern with increasing appropriateness the
courses of action that will most effectively mirror divine
attributes of justice and mercy. Unless individuals
consciences are cultivated, however, there can be little
hope for a just order.

The Qur'an mediates the speech of God to humanity;
some passages are also used by individuals when they speak
back to God in prayer. The language of the sacred book
thus shapes and reshapes the consciousness of the believer
who tries continually to refashion and reorder his or her
thoughts and practices in the direction indicated by
revelation. Just as a Christian steeped in the Psalms of
David might answer the question "Who are you?" with the
reply, "The Lord is my Shepherd, I shall not want" (Psalm
23), so a devout Muslim may base his or her sense of
identity on the verses of Surah Fatiha, which are then used
daily in prayer.

> Praise belongs to God, the Lord of all Being,
> the All-merciful, the All-compassionate
> the Master of the Day of Doom.
> Thee only we serve; to Thee alone we pray for
>   succour.
> Guide us in the straight path,
> the path of those whom Thou hast blessed
> not of those against whom Thou are wrathful,
>   nor of those who are astray.[12]

The Muslim's answer to this question of identity is that
one affirms one's existence in praising the Lord of all
Being, in serving God alone, and in seeking guidance in
following the straight path of those who have been blessed.
The blessing in the first instance is the guidance that has
been given through the prophets, and finally through the
Prophet Muhammad.

Boisard in his book L'Humanisme de l'Islam has used
the terms equality, equity, and equilibrium to indicate
three fundamental characteristics of Muslim ethical
thought.[13] The egalitarianism of Islam stems from the

basic relationships of each person with God: each is
ultimately responsible to God alone. He or she prays
daily, "Thee only we serve." The person thus praying
knows that no kings, priests, or other authorities can
stand between human beings and their Creator. The
traditions of courtesy and good manners that have
characterized many Islamic civilizations have arisen in
part because of the basic requirement that each person has
his or her own dignity and must be treated graciously.[14]

Equity indicates that the justice which humans seek to
implement in their social organizations must be based on an
on-going effort to realize in human terms that justice
which is an attribute of God. The straight path that is
the goal of human life is usually characterized by Muslim
thinkers as the middle way between extremes. It is also
the path that reflects most closely the divine attributes.
Justice should always be tempered by mercy, since human
attempts at implementing righteousness will necessarily be
finite and inadequate. Justice and mercy are both
attributes of God. The responsibility each person bears
towards God is the core that shapes the conscience of that
individual. He or she must decide in practice which
decisions will most adequately reflect the attributes of
God.

Equilibrium is also a fundamental characteristic of
the Muslim way of perceiving the relationship of human
beings to the universe as a whole. Some studies of Islamic
art and architecture have indicated iconoclasm, the refusal
to portray human beings or animals, as well as an interest
in abstract patterns. This latter interest has led to the
elaboration of complex abstractions that indicate a
perceived interrelatedness of all forms. Harmony and
balance have been major characteristics of Islamic art.[15]
This awareness of equilibrium, suggested in the work of
artists, has also shaped the thinking of jurists and others
who have been concerned to design social forms.

We have noted that discontinuity occurs between
medieval and modern Muslims in a number of respects. It
occurs with respect to the Qur'an: individuals can and do

read the Qur'an for themselves, and they tend to exercise
private judgment about what the scriptures mean. There is
also discontinuity in relation to the medieval
understanding of the hierarchical nature of the cosmos.
Earlier forms of ethical writing assumed that the
perfecting of the self involved a movement of
self-awareness from a lower to a higher plane. This
notion of hierarchy has tended to disappear from modern
Muslim thought.

The cumulative tradition of ethical thinking in Islam
also includes principles of jurisprudence.[16] Modern
ethical thinkers, such as the two men we discuss are aware
that most Muslims assume that a pattern of life had been
established by the earlier Muslim jurists--a pattern of
life generally understood as normative. A major problem,
therefore, when one deals with the discontinuity caused by
modernization, has been how to think about changes in the
pattern. The modern ethical thinkers have been concerned
to legitimate the changes they deem necessary.

The legitimation of change can be accomplished by
appeals to reason, to scripture, and to exemplars. As we
shall see later, the rationalist and the fundamentalist
ethical thinkers use all three modes of persuading their
co-religionists to change life and thought. The appeal to
reason in itself requires justification; one of the
widespread assumptions of the medieval period was that no
further intellectual effort was required, other than
submission to authoritative opinion (taqlid). The
assumption was that, by the tenth century, all necessary
original thinking had been done. This assumption is
usually expressed by the statement that the gates of
ijtihad (fresh thinking) had been closed. One recent
scholar has pointed out that the belief in the closing of
the gate is not based on firm evidence. "Nobody quite
knows when the 'gate of ijtihad' was closed or who exactly
closed it....There is no statement to be found anywhere by
anyone about the desirability or the necessity of such a
closure, or of the fact of actually closing the gate,
although one finds judgments by later writers that the

'gate of ijtihad' has been closed."[17]   In effect, then, the
closing of the gate was a myth; no jurist had ever closed
it. It served as an effective myth, however, in providing
stability and uniformity.

I use religious-legal as a translation for fiqh, which
is sometimes translated as the science of jurisprudence,
because the content of the religious law, shari'a, which
was worked out by the Muslim jurists, deals with that
behaviour which is necessary in the light of revelation.
In other words, persons learn from the shari'a how to
participate in the religious rituals as well as how to
order personal and collective lives. Life is to be shaped
in response to what God has said and required. Problems
arose very early: Muslims found themselves, within one
hundred years of the death of the Prophet Muhammad, rulers
and administrators of vast territories that had formerly
been under Sassanian Persian or Byzantine Christian
administration. Muslims believed that they owed their
success to God's gracious self-revelation of his nature and
purposes to them. They saw themselves as required to
respond to this divine mercy by elaborating and
implementing a way of life that would be acceptable to God.

But how? The phrase "religious-legal" encompasses the
efforts made both to insure the integrity of personal
religious life by upholding the virtues of sincerity and
humility, and to develop judicial and other structures that
would facilitate the implementation of social justice.
Jurists and administrators had to decide all manner of
practical matters with little to guide them save their
knowledge of the Qur'an, the example of the Prophet and his
early Companions, existing administrative practices, and
reason. The problems were compounded in the early days by
the relative lack of Islamic precedents and by the physical
difficulties of knowing what other Muslims were doing in
the vast territories that made up the Muslim world.

Some rationalist and fundamentalist debates in the
modern period focus on the question of whether, and in what
sense, reason had been used in this early period to decide
how to implement revelation. One recent study of the

methodology of the early phases of Islamic legal thinking
has emphasized that the use of reason had been essential in
the first instance. Fazlur Rahman has explained how the
theoretical idea of the Prophet's example, sunna,
originally functioned:

> We have said that the early Islamic literature
> strongly suggests that the Prophet was not a
> pan-legist. For one thing, it can be concluded
> a priori that the Prophet, who was, until his
> death, engaged in a grim moral and political
> struggle against the Meccans and the Arabs and
> in organizing his community-state, could hardly
> have found time to lay down rules for minutiae
> of life. Indeed, the Muslim community went
> about its normal business settling disputes by
> themselves in the light of common sense and on
> the basis of their customs which, after certain
> modifications, were left intact by the Prophet.
> It was only in cases that became especially
> acute that the Prophet was called upon to decide
> and in certain cases the Qur'an had to intervene.
> Mostly such cases were of an ad hoc nature, and
> were treated informally and in an ad hoc manner.
> Thus, these cases could be taken as normative
> prophetic examples and quasi-precedents but not
> strictly and literally.
> . . . . That the Prophetic Sunnah was a general
> umbrella-concept rather than filled with an
> absolutely specific content flows directly, at
> a theoretical level, from the fact that the
> Sunnah is a behavioural term: since no two
> cases, in practice, are ever exactly identical
> in their situational setting--moral,
> psychological and material--Sunnah, must, of
> necessity, allow of interpretation and
> adaptation. But quite apart from this
> theoretical analysis, there is abundant
> historical evidence to show that this was
> actually the case . . .
> The necessary instrument whereby the Prophetic
> model was progressively developed into a definite
> and specific code of human behaviour by the early
> generations of Muslims was responsible free
> thought activity. . . . But with all its wealth,
> the product of this activity became rather
> chaotic.[18]

As a result of this chaos, the notion of sunna came to
have the meaning of agreed practice, rather than exemplary
precedent. This change of meaning came about through the
process of ijma, the consensus of the scholar-jurists.
Fazlur Rahman has commented on an aphorism from the second
Islamic century: "'The Sunnah decides upon the Qur'an; the
Qur'an does not decide the Sunnah' . . . . What the

aphorism means is <u>that the Community, under the direction</u>
<u>of the spirit (not the absolute letter) in which the</u>
<u>Prophet acted in a given historical situation, shall</u>
<u>authoritatively interpret and assign meaning to</u>
<u>Revelation</u>."[19] He gives an example. The Qur'an had said
that for a decision two males, or one male and two females
would be required to give evidence. In the established
actual practice, however, civil cases were decided on the
basis of one witness plus an oath. And this was justified
by the founder of one of the major schools of Islamic law,
Imam Malik (d. 795).

In terms of the principles of jurisprudence, the
tendency to restrict or to eliminate individual judgment
came later. The jurist al-Shafi (d. 820) is credited with
having formalized the principles of jurisprudence which
served as the basis for the <u>shari'a</u> throughout the
medieval period. He stated as his primary principle the
maxim that justice is nothing but obedience to law.[20]

Fazlur Rahman considers this development to have been
unfortunate for the long-range development of the community
in his comments regarding <u>Ijma</u> (consensus):

It is clear that al-Shafi's notion of <u>Ijma</u> was
radically different from that of the early
schools. His idea of <u>Ijma</u> was that of a
formal and a total one; he demanded an
agreement which left no room for disagreement.
He was undoubtedly responding to the
exigencies of the time and was but a
monumental representative of a trend that had
long set in, working towards equilibrium and
uniformity. . . . <u>Ijma</u>, instead of being a
process and something forward-looking--came to
be something static and backward looking. It
is that which, instead of having to be
accomplished, is already accomplished in the
past. Al-Shafi's genius provided a mechanism
that gave stability to our medieval
socio-religious fabric but at the cost, in the
long run, of creativity and originality.[21]

Thus within the discipline of religious-legal thinking, the
emphasis after al-Shafi came to be on upholding an
agreed-upon pattern as authoritative. This process meant
that a particular interpretation of revelation was accorded
priority over reason. The jurists themselves did not give
much thought or attention to the basic question of whether

the right and the good could be known by reason. They left
these theoretical problems to theology, kalam.

George Hourani, in a discussion of the early debates
that arose between Muslim theologians on the issue of the
role of reason in determining values, has characterized the
two points of view that dominated the discussions as
rationalistic objectivism and theistic subjectivism.[22]
Those in the first group, known as the Mu'tazila, asserted
the efficacy of natural reason as a source of ethical
knowledge. Their position, as indicated in the writings of
Abd al-Jabbar (c. 935-1025), was that the power of God was
not limited in any way that matters by the existence of
rational human judgments of value.[23] Their opponents, the
Asharites, took the contrary view, maintaining that God's
power could not be shared: only God could decide what was
right and good; values could only be known through
revelation. The consequence of the position of the
Asharites was a legitimation of the all-embracing divine
law which had just been worked out by the jurists.

Hourani maintains that the debates between these two
schools of thought was distinctive, and owed little to any
outside influence. He comments:

> The sustained discussion on ethics in the kalam
> literature is all the more remarkable because
> it owes little to the Greeks except in an
> indirect and diffuse way. It is original in
> Islam, and grew naturally out of the early
> theological and juristic debates among Muslims.
> It appears to me as chronologically the second
> major occurrence in history of a profound
> discussion on the meaning and general content
> of ethical concepts, the first being that of
> the ancient Greek sophists and Plato.[24]

Hourani uses the term theistic subjectivism to
characterise the stance of al-Ashari: "It is subjectivism
because the value of action is defined by relation to
certain attitudes or opinions of a mind in the position of
judge or observer, such as wishing and not wishing,
commanding and forbidding, approving and disapproving. It
is theistic because the mind is that of God, in contrast
with human subjectivism of various types."[25] Thus the
goodness or badness of any action can be understood solely
in terms of whether God approves or disapproves of it. God

had commanded children to respect their parents. He had
forbidden gambling. From the theistic subjectivist
position, attitudes and actions of this kind cannot be
rationally defended or taught in any way other than by
demanding that believers accept them.

Although it was the theologians who explicitly
defended this position, the same point of view also
informed the perspective of many of the jurists:

> Shafi'i carried on an unrelenting polemic
> against the use of personal judgment in
> law unsupported by revelational authority
> of any kind. Against it he urged that
> although such judgement aims to know what
> is right through reason, it is in fact
> mere arbitrary opinion, often erroneous,
> easily led astray by desires and
> prejudices, and lacking authority as a
> source of law. 'Does man reckon that he
> shall be left to roam at random?'
> (Qur'an lxxv. 36). Shafi'i interprets:
> 'Left to roam at random' means 'one who
> is not commanded or prohibited.'...The
> implication of his jurisprudence is
> either that there are objective ethical
> values but man's reason cannot know them,
> or that the only ethical values derive
> from divine commands. That in fact he
> held the latter view is shown by his
> definition 'Justice is acting in
> obedience to God' and other statements to
> the same effect. Thus, without stating a
> theory of ethics, Shafi'i foreshadowed
> and led to the theistic subjectivism of
> the traditional theologians.[26]

Al-Ashari emphasized in his theological system the
transcendent omnipotence of God as contrasted with the
fragility and powerlessness of human beings. Power seems
to have been his major preoccupation. In ethics, this
meant that God was not limited in any way by human notions
of appropriate behaviour. If God were to be limited, he
would be weak. Thus al-Ashari argued that absolute power
was a prerequisite for God.

Although the Mu'tazila had been initially prior to the
Asharites, the dispute between the two theological schools
went on for several generations. Abd al-Jabbar (d. 1024)
was a prominent jurist and theologian who was considered
the head of the Mu'tazilite school in his generation: he
died approximately one hundred years later than al-Ashari.

His viewpoint thus indicates a Mu'tazilite perspective
which had acknowledged the Asharite critique, and which had
yet retained its own distinctive outlook. He holds that
everyone can know such general ethical truths as "wrong
doing is evil" immediately by intuitive reason.[27] He
claims that there is always an intelligible reason for the
things prohibited and commanded in revelation, accessible
in principle to our intelligence. Abd al-Jabbar quotes the
Qur'an to support this view: "Surely God bids to justice
and good-doing and giving to kinsmen; and He forbids
indecency, dishonour and insolence" (Qur'an. xvl. 92).

These Mu'tazila scholars thought that no serious
conflict existed between revelation and reason because
revelation encourages devout persons to do what they know
to be good and to refrain from what they know to be evil.
The Qur'an thus serves to motivate and to encourage persons
in their struggles to become the just and good persons that
they know they ought to be. If acts were good only because
God says so, and not because of their intrinsic worth, God
could punish prophets, reward Pharoah, tell lies, and order
useless acts. If there were no human standards of value,
there would be no basis from which humans could genuinely
appreciate and value God's goodness. One might say that
Abd al-Jabbar's religious seriousness takes the form of
insistence that a genuine response to God requires that the
believer have the capacity truly to appreciate and to be
grateful for the goodness of God.

Abd al-Jabbar argues that there are objective ethical
concepts in the Qur'an. Such evils are wrongdoing (injury
to another person), uselessness, lying, ingratitude for a
favour, ignorance, willing evil, and commanding evil.
People commonly do evil because of self-interest. The
importance of revelation lies in motivating believers to
transcend their self-interest and to cultivate pure souls.
Evil is a real possibility, and persons can know that they
are doing evil when they lie or harm others. The Qur'an
confirms that these forms of behaviour are evil and greatly
strengthens the will to abstain from evil and to do good.
Once believers know that God is supportive of their efforts

to do good, their wills will be strengthened and sustained.

The position described above went into relative
obscurity in the years following Abd al-Jabbar. These were
centuries of internal disruptions in the Muslim community.
The Mongol invasions devastated large parts of the Muslim
world. Recovery took several centuries. The emphasis on
taqlid, acceptance of authority, meant that little further
innovative work was done in the areas of jurisprudence or
theology. There were a few outstanding individual
thinkers, notably Ibn Taymiyah and Ibn Khaldun in the
fourteenth century, but they did not establish major and
effective schools of thought. Their ideas became
influential centuries later.

The rationalist and fundamentalist ethical thinkers of
the modern period who are looking for precedents and
exemplars tend to look back to the earliest phase of
Islamic history, the period of the first four Caliphs, and
to the founders of the schools of religious-legal thought.
When the modern thinkers concern themselves with issues
related to principles of jurisprudence, they have of
necessity to deal with the question of the role of reason
in interpreting revelation. We shall see in the following
chapters how each thinker justifies his own understanding
of reason in the light of his interpretation of the
processes whereby Muslims arrive at consensus. Neither the
Muslim rationalist of the modern period nor the
fundamentalist accepts taqlid. Both of them acknowledge in
their own ways the discontinuity in Muslim life and thought
caused by the disappearance of the medieval political and
social structures; further, they recognize that the
intellectual challenge occasioned by the new forms of
knowledge being transmitted through the universities
requires fresh and original thinking.

Throughout our discussion, we will assume that ethical
thinking means a concern with ideal human virtues, as well
as an interest in how to develop and to maintain good
structures. These structures include family life, as well
as social, economic, political, and religious patterns,
including ritual. Muslims generally assume that every

aspect of existence is lived under the guidance of God.
Hence all human activity should be related to divine
wisdom.

In the cumulative tradition of Muslim ethical
thinking, much of the most influential writing about human
virtues and potentialities was done by philosophers and
sufis (mystics). Philosophers are not generally respected
by Muslims as significant exemplars; much of their
writing, especially with respect to cosmology, was
considered too foreign. With respect to ethics, however,
the writings of some of the philosophers have been
influential. The eleventh-century philosopher, Ibn
Miskiwaih, wrote a volume entitled Tadhib ul Akhlaq, which
has been, and continues to be, read by Muslims as a guide
to the procedures to be used for training virtuous
character. Tadhib ul Akhlaq has been translated as The
Refinement of Character. When we come to consider the
modern rationalist thinker Sayyid Ahmad Khan, we will see
that writings such as this treatise of Ibn Miskiwaih seem
to have influenced his thinking.

Ibn Mishiwaih's stance was that of a member of a
cultured elite of administrators. He had behind him the
Persian as well as the Byzantine administrative tradition,
yet he was a devout Muslim. The good man, from his
perspective, was a responsible person, one who used good
judgment and balance in the affairs of office. Such good
men would have to be trained in the virtues of self-
discipline and patient self-control. There is little trace
of gnostic world rejection in Ibn Miskiwaih's ethical
thinking. The person was to be trained in virtue so that
he might be enabled to act constructively with other
persons for the good of the community as a whole. The
training in self-control should begin with the young child:
"The boy should be made to despise the value of food, which
gluttonous people extol, and to disdain those who covet it
and take more of it than is necessary for their bodies or
indulge in what does not agree with them."[28] The child
must learn to stare at other people's food and generally to
exercise what is probably the most basic of all the forms

of self-control and moderation. Ibn Mishkiwaih's
relationship to Islam is perhaps best exemplified by the
praise he gives to the ritual and social practices
inculcated by the Muslim tradition.

> You must realize that this fellowship innate
> in man is the (value) that we must be eager
> to keep and to acquire in common with our
> fellow men. We must exert our efforts and
> our capacities so as to not miss achieving
> it, because it is the origin of all kinds of
> love. It is indeed to help develop this
> fellowship that both the Law and good custom
> have enjoined people to invite one another
> and to meet five times a day in their
> mosques and preferred communal prayer to
> individual prayer in order that they may
> experience this inborn fellowship which is
> the origin of all love and which exists in
> them in potency. In this way, this inborn
> fellowship would become actual, and would
> then be strengthened by the right beliefs
> which bind them together.29

Ibn Miskiwaih expected that what is truly good would be
supported by both the law, shari'a, and good custom.

Sufism is Muslim mysticism. From the twelfth to the
nineteenth centuries, sufism comprehensively pervaded
Muslim society.30 Sufi orders were present and active in
every part of the Muslim world. The centres of the orders
served often as local shrines, or places where believers
could come to take part in ritual devotional exercises, or
to find spiritual counselling. The sufis became something
like the spiritual conscience of the Muslim peoples. They
became the authorities on matters such as the maturation of
the self and the cultivation of the virtues which would
enable individuals to feel that they had come close to
God.31

The sufi contribution to ethics stressed the necessity
of inner integrity. Since sufism is concerned with the
disciplines of personal purification, training the will and
the attitudes, the emphasis is more on inner states than on
conforming to external norms or patterns of behaviour.
Sufis tended to emphasize practice rather than abstract
theory. From the sufi point of view, self-knowledge and
self-purification are necessary preconditions to a more
perfect knowledge of God. The self has to be cleansed of

false pride, anger, and greed. The sufi virtues are
patience and sobriety. The great sufi writer al-Ghazali
(d. 1111) has been one of the most influential Muslim
writers on ethics. An example of his stance is as follows:

> First examine your own condition and if you
> find there one blameworthy thing then be
> tolerant of what you see in your brother. .
> . . So do not be too heavy on him on
> account of one blameworthy trait--what man
> is completely upright? Wherever you find
> yourself lacking in your duty to God, do
> not expect as much from your brother in his
> duty to you, for your right over him is not
> greater than God's right over you. . . .
>
> Second, you know that were you to seek for
> someone free of all blemish you would
> exhaust the entire Creation without ever
> finding a companion. For there is not one
> human being who does not have both good
> qualities and bad, and if the good outweigh
> the bad that is the most that can be hoped
> for.
>
> The noble believer always keeps present in
> himself the good qualities of his brother,
> so that his heart may be the source of
> honour, affection and respect. As for the
> hypocrite of low character, he is always
> noticing misdeeds and faults. . . .
>
> This is why the Prophet (God bless him and
> give him Peace) said:
> --Seek refuge with God from the bad
> neighbour who sees some good and conceals
> it, sees some bad and reveals it.
>
> There is no-one at all whose condition
> cannot be improved in some respects, or
> made worse. . . .
>
> The source of deficiency in veiling
> another's shame, and of striving to
> display it, is a hidden disease of the
> Inner, namely rancour and envy. For the
> rancorous and envious has his inner full of
> dirt, but keeps it imprisoned in his Inner,
> conceals it and does not show it as long as
> he lacks a pretext. But when he finds an
> opportunity the restraint is released, the
> reserve is abandoned, and the Inner sweats
> with its hidden dirt. . . .

Ibn Abbas reported the Messenger of God
(God bless him and give him Peace) as
saying:
--Do not dispute with your brother, do not
mock him, and do not go back on your
promise to him.

He (God bless him and give him Peace) also
said:
--You will not win people with your
wealth. What will win them is a cheerful
face and a good character. . . .

Someone said that patience with the pain
caused by a brother is better than
rebuking him in return, though rebuke is
better than breaking off and breaking off
is better than back-biting. . . . God
(Exalted is He) said:
--Perhaps God will create affection
between you and those you have had as
enemies. (Qur'an 60.7).[32]

The phrase "for your right over him is not greater
than God's right over you" is a very important instance of
Muslim ethical seriousness. The individual's personal,
emotional reactions to the behaviour of others, his hurt
feelings, his jealousy, should be disregarded as much as
possible. From this sufi perspective, the well-being of
others takes priority over the needs of the individual.
The reason is that the individual is to trust in God and
not to be overly preoccupied with his or her own condition.
The virtues are thus seen to flourish as part of an
on-going process whereby the intentions of the individual
are increasingly directed away from preoccupation with
self. Religious development is a process of maturation.
The virtues flower as the self develops. Therefore the
structures of society are to be ordered so that all
possible obstacles to the full blossoming of human
potential can be removed. The end of existence is to bear
witness to the attributes of God.

Ethical thinking for Muslims thus ranges over many
kinds of concerns. It includes maturation, as in
al-Ghazali, and an interest in moral training, as in Ibn
Miskiwaih. It also covers the intellectual procedures of
the scholars concerned with principles of jurisprudence and
the interest of the theologians in discussing the

relationship of reason to revelation. This is by no means
an exhaustive list, but it serves to highlight some
concerns particularly relevant to issues dealt with in the
writings of Muslim thinkers concerned with modernity,
allowing us to move on to the more detailed discussion of
the ethical thinking of the two modern Muslims in
question.

Sayyid Ahmad Khan (1817-1898):
Islamic Rationalist

I have chosen the writings of Sayyid Ahmad Khan as
illustrative of the main characteristics of the rationalist
position in modern (that is, post-1800) Muslim ethical
thinking. Sayyid Ahmad Khan was one of the first and most
significant representatives of those Muslims who perceived
clearly that the impact of the scientific and industrial
revolutions would necessarily disrupt traditional Muslim
society. He was self-consciously an ethicist because he
believed that the most effective way to make a constructive
adjustment to new challenges would be through a critical
discussion of values.

    He was born and raised in an aristocratic Muslim
family in Mughal Delhi. He thus imbibed the courtly
traditions of courtesy and diplomacy from his early youth.
His maternal grandfather had been a scholar of mathematics
as well as a diplomat who served in Iran. Traditional
Muslim science was part of his heritage. As a young man,
Sayyid Ahmad wrote a treatise refuting the notion of the
earth revolving around the sun, but he later changed his
opinion on this matter.

    He also exhibited in early life an interest in the
history of his immediate community, the Muslims of Delhi.
He wrote a history of the distinguished personalities of
Delhi. He also devoted himself to a study of the
architecture and archeological remains of the city. One
catches a glimpse of his personal qualities from a
narrative that describes him hanging in a basket from the
top of the immensely high Qutb Minar attempting to decipher
inscriptions.[1] The courage, imaginativeness, and
resourcefulness indicated by that incident were to be
demonstrated again and again during the tumultuous events
of his active life. He was later made a Fellow of the
Royal Asiatic Society for his archeological researches in
Delhi.

Sayyid Ahmad Khan's training and interest in science
and history were qualities he had gained from exposure to
the cultured life of the aristocratic elite of Mughal
Delhi. These qualities stood him in good stead when later
in life he had to deal with the English. He owed nothing
in the first instance to foreign influence. His supreme
self-confidence in his own cultural roots was the
profoundest source of his creativeness--one might say that
he thought Muslims could do anything and that nothing human
was foreign to them. He continued throughout his long life
to meet the impact of the new with lively curiosity and
ready interest. In attempting to disentangle the issues of
rationalism in ethics, it is important to bear in mind
that, in Sayyid Ahmad Khan's case, rationalism meant in
part the distinguishing characteristic of a good scientist,
historian, diplomat, or judge.

His own profession was that of a magistrate
(sub-judge) in the British service in India. Legal and
ethical problems were practical matters to him. His ideas
about social change did not come from an ivory tower of
academic contemplation, or from mystical insight into
utopian possibilities, but rather from immediate contact
with the real disorders and conflicts of his environment.
He was an avid reader of newspapers, a man always urgently
concerned to try to understand the realities of given
situations. He used the discipline acquired from science
and history when he thought and wrote on ethical questions.
His rationalism was linked to the dispassionate objectivity
necessary for sound scholarship. A mind of this quality
tends to be able to meet the new openly and to consider its
viability freely without succumbing to debilitating
emotional shock.

When he travelled to England in 1869, Sayyid Ahmad
Khan wrote home. From these letters, we can see how
busily his mind was at work observing everywhere how things
were done:

>From the cursory view of Egypt which I got I
>was astonished. . . . Its land seems to be
>splendidly manured, and the canals with
>their branches are innumerable. . . .

> The special train that took us across Egypt
> consisted of first and second class, . . the
> second class in which my servant Chajju sat,
> being superior to those in use in India, they
> having leather cushions. . . . The
> engine-drivers, guards, and attendants are
> all Egyptian or Turks, and are well up in
> their work and very careful. . . . There is
> certainly one thing in favour of the
> Egyptians, contrasted with natives of India--
> i.e. that they can use . . . materials, which
> my unfortunate fellow-countrymen cannot. The
> reason why the Egyptians can do this is, that
> all the scientific words necessary have been
> brought into use in their language, and this
> must be the case with us before we can rise
> to their level. . . .
> One great pleasure to me on board . . . was
> meeting M. de Lesseps, who, as all the world
> knows, is the maker of the Suez Canal, and
> who, although many of the first engineers of
> the age asserted the impossibility of its
> being made, stuck to his firm belief . . .
> and said he would do it himself. He did it,
> and has now united two oceans. M. de Lesseps
> was most kind to me. . . . I was delighted to
> find that he spoke a little Arabic and conversed
> with him to some extent in that language. From
> that day he always met me cordially and we sat
> for hours daily at the same table writing. . . .
> It was a very great pleasure and honour to me to
> meet a man whose determination and pluck were
> equal to his science, and who has not his equal
> in the whole world.[2]

This quotation serves well to indicate Sayyid Ahmad's
basic attitude. He was always particularly pleased to
discover Muslims who knew their jobs and who did them well.
He spent a lot of time talking with the Muslim pilot of the
ship on this part of the trip. The comment about the
workers on the train is typical. His admiration for de
Lesseps shows that he valued highly a man who was able
through his disciplined intelligence to solve a serious
problem, and who then had the persistence and the courage
to implement his ideas in the face of criticism, abuse, and
disbelief from others. The emphasis on the necessity of
having scientific works available in one's own language is
also characteristic. Sayyid Ahmad Khan spent a good deal
of energy organizing societies to translate works into Urdu
for the benefit of Indian Muslims.

His rationality as a diplomat also had Islamic roots.

One aspect of the Prophet Muhammad's career was his
success in mediating disputes and in reconciling former
opponents. Sayyid Ahmad's maternal grandfather had been a
diplomat. The Mughal court with which his family had been
associated had a background of many generations of
traditional wisdom on the necessity of cultivated manners
in solving problems between people. Sayyid Ahmad's
biographers say that his mother strongly influenced his
training in these respects. She taught him to treat
servants well and never to respond to vituperation with
anger or malice.[3] Throughout his long life he was
subjected to a great deal of abuse; it is a matter of
public record that his responses were not characterized by
personal vindictiveness.

In Sayyid Ahmad's role as a diplomat he was concerned
to mediate between the Indian Muslims and their English
rulers, to remove obstacles of misunderstanding that caused
friction, and to smooth the path for good relations between
them. The English control over most of India was a
political reality that Sayyid Ahmad acknowledged regardless
of personal bias or opinion. His concern was to discover
how the English had achieved their superiority and then to
teach his people how to reach the same levels of
effectiveness in the world. One Englishman commented that
Sayyid Ahmad was the arch-rebel; he taught his people how
to play the games of the English and then how to beat them
at those very games.[4]

Sayyid Ahmad's rationality as an historian was
similar. His response to the disaster of the 1857 Revolt
had been to write about it. The History of the Bijnore
Rebellion is his account of his personal experiences in the
district where he was stationed as he remained loyal to the
English and tried to restore order into a chaotic
situation. His life was certainly in danger there,
although he comments that his people did not need to fear
the artillery in the hands of the mutineers since they
rarely hit the targets:

     I feel a sincere need at this point to say
     something about the artillery. The
     artillery and artillery men . . . were of

> such a caliber that if the Himalaya Mountains
> were to stand in place of their usual targets
> . . . they would always miss the target. . .
> . On the day of his defeat . . . the
> artillerymen of the Nawab must have fired no
> less than 17 times at a building where the
> Deputy and I were staying. But they did not
> scare us a bit, although they had a clear
> range of fire and ample time to take most
> careful aim. When we began to fire on them
> from this house, with our . . . muskets, they
> removed the battery from directly opposite
> the house. I can swear that not one man will
> die in all this fighting from an artillery
> ball.[5]

This resembles the earlier reference to de Lesseps. Sayyid
Ahmad always noted competence in the use of equipment and
in solving problems. As he saw it, the persons agitating
in the revolt were futile because of their incompetence.
The mutiny in general would not solve the problems of his
generation.

Rationality, however, does not preclude passion. The
destruction of Delhi by the English after the failure of
the mutiny was a matter of great personal grief to him.
Nevertheless, his discipline was such that he responded to
the crisis as a diplomat and as an historian, writing for
the English a dispassionate analysis of the reasons why, in
his view, the disaster had occurred.[6]

While Sayyid Ahmad's admiration for certain aspects of
Western civilization was by no means unqualified, his
criticism of his own people could be severe. "I lamented
the degeneracy of my own race, who are, as a rule, steeped
in envy and all uncharitableness, and saw only too plainly
that by such bad habits they are dishonoured and
unfortunate."[7] But he could also comment on the English.
"The English are the cleanest of nations, although some of
their customs are open to cavil."[8] In particular, he
disliked the drinking. He notes the bad manners of an
English passenger who wrote in an autograph book, "'the
natives of India are heartless and ungrateful'."[9] This
kind of contempt in Sayyid Ahmad Khan's view, was
dangerous; it led to anger and violence among those
despised. In his study of the causes of the 1857 Revolt,
he attributed most of the blame to the incompetence of the

English as rulers. They were ineffective because their
bigoted and self-satisfied arrogance prevented them from
assessing accurately the needs of those they governed. By
the standards of Muslim notions of effective government,
the British made serious mistakes because of stupidity and
racism.

Tahzib-ul-Akhlaq

When Sayyid Ahmad Khan returned from England in 1870,
he and his associates began the publication of the journal
entitled Tahzib-ul-Akhlaq in Urdu; the English subtitle was
The Muhammadan Social Reformer. Although a more accurate
English translation would have been something like The
Refinement of Character, it was Sayyid Ahmad's own choice
to phrase the subtitle as indicated. Perhaps he was
consciously urging the idea that refinement of character
and social reform were closely linked. In the first issue
of the journal, he explained that the purpose was to
encourage reform and progress in the Muslim community in
India. The background of this journal was both the
philosophical tradition of Islamic ethical thought and the
reformist tradition in European ethics--from Montaigne and
Montesquieu through Addison and Steele.

The link with the Muslim philosophical past is obvious
in the traditional Urdu title. Sayyid Ahmad had devoted a
good deal of his time to studying medieval Muslim
philosophical, theological, and legal writings, and he saw
his own efforts as a continuation of a tradition. His
mind-set was very like that of his eleventh-century
predecessor, Ibn Miskiwaih: both were active participants
in cultured, governing elites; and both published writings
in science and history as well as in ethics. Among other
concerns, Sayyid Ahmad had been interested in technical
competence; Ibn Miskiwaih had been interested in problems
of agricultural reform. Both exemplify the general
effectiveness of Muslim administrators from the beginnings
of their civilization.

Sayyid Ahmad Khan, of course, had facilities such as

the printing press available to him that were quite
different from those at the disposal of Ibn Miskiwaih. The
phenomenon of religious journalism has been widespread and
very important in India in the years since Sayyid Ahmad
Khan, for he was the first Indian Muslim to use this
religious journalism with great effectiveness as a way of
persuading his fellow believers to think about values and
practices.

     He used insights from medieval ethical thinkers, but
he discarded the hierarchical cosmology which underlay the
medieval concepts of the self. In his view, many of these
outmoded Greek conceptions had to be discarded if Muslims
were to be able to think effectively. We noted that he
personally endured the mental struggle of first defending
and then finally rejecting, in the light of the new
evidence, the medieval Muslim picture of the cosmos. He
thus knew that a process of sorting out which traditional
materials were still useful, and which were not, would have
to be undertaken by the members of the community as a
whole.

     Sayyid Ahmad Khan was concerned to preserve valid
insight while rejecting outmoded cosmology. Fazlur Rahman
has noted that only two medieval scholars had insisted
that, in the matter of deciding which persons were
qualified to become mujtahid (qualified to exercise
ijtihad) training in rational disciplines, the capacity to
make deductions was a prerequisite that came before Islamic
scholarship. These two were al-Ghazali and Fakhr al-Din
al-Razi,[10] generally acknowledged as two of the greatest
Muslim religious and ethical thinkers. One can certainly
reasonably suggest that Sayyid Ahmad Khan was following the
lead of these two, and rejecting the guidance of all the
others who did not see the need for training in rational
disciplines.

     He believed that the social thought of Western
ethicists, such as Montaigne, Montesquieu, Addison, and
Steele, had helped the process of transforming Western
societies towards structures through which greater
well-being had become possible for many more members of the

community.[11] Ethical thinking could be, he thought, a
powerful instrument of social change. Therefore, he used
the English subtitle The Muhammadan Social Reformer to
indicate his intention to urge serious change.

Sayyid Ahmad Khan did not think of cultural systems as
fixed entities. He rather envisaged them as processes. He
thought that the European societies in the preceding two
centuries had undergone many phases of social
transformation. He saw no reason why the Muslim societies
should not also undergo similar forms of transformation
which would lead to greater well-being for the members of
the community. In brief, Muslims might take to sitting on
chairs and eating at tables for their meals, but that did
not mean they would have to drink wine and to eat pork.
The problem for the ethical thinkers was precisely to sort
out on behalf of the community, those aspects of social
belief and practice that could usefully be discarded in the
interests of greater hygiene and efficiency from those
basic to the community's moral strength and integrity. If
modernizing were to turn pious Muslims into alcoholics, the
purposes of Sayyid Ahmad Khan's reforms would not have been
effective.

His English friend Graham wrote a biography of Sayyid
Ahmad Khan intended to help change English attitudes of
contempt and hostility towards Muslims. The English had
become much more contemptuous of Indians in the nineteenth
century than they had been in preceding centuries. The
presence of many English women in India had helped to
increase the antagonism and distance between the two
communities. Graham invited Sayyid Ahmad Khan to a private
dinner party at which Graham's wife was present. This was,
Graham says, the first time that an Indian Muslim had
attended a private dinner party where English women were
present. Subsequently, Mrs. Graham was given a meal at
Sayyid Ahmad Khan's home. Graham recorded the event.

> After an excellent English dinner some attendants
> brought in a large package, wrapped in scarlet
> cloth, and sealed with the Imperial seal of
> Delhi. When opened the package was found to
> contain thirty or more dishes of real Mohammedan
> cookery, prepared and cooked by the begums of the

Princess of Delhi, then living at Benares, and
sealed as in the time of the old Emperors of
Delhi; a wise protection against poison. Some
of the dishes were excellent, and Syed Ahmad
was greatly pleased at my wife's appreciation
of them, for whom them had been prepared.[12]

This exchange of food, and particularly Mrs. Graham's
eating of the food appropriate to the Muslim aristocrats
of Delhi, is symbolic of Sayyid Ahmad Khan's understanding
of the processes that were necessary for the transformation
of his people's condition in the world. The understanding
that the sharing of food is an expression of mutual
acceptance and recognition of bonds of mutual support is a
fundamental Islamic idea; hospitality to guests is a basic
Muslim virtue. If courtesy as a guest required eating with
new instruments, it should be done. The significant point
is that it is the human quality of the relationship between
hosts and guests that is important, not the issue of what
instruments are to be used. Islam is a religious tradition
that stresses sacred reality as a quality of human
relationships rather than as a substance residing in dishes
and other utensils. From this perspective, it would be
un-Islamic to think of oneself as polluted by any kind of
material object; .Islam had demystified objects as bearers
of sacred power.

That Sayyid Ahmad Khan wanted the English to
acknowledge the validity of his cultural tradition is
indicated by his pleasure in Mrs. Graham's enjoyment of his
people's food. His effort was directed towards changing
English manners as well as Muslim ones. The English woman
who might have refused Muslim food would have been
contemptible to him as a narrow-minded bigot.

In an article entitled "Culture," Sayyid Ahmad Khan
urged his fellow Muslims to acquire critical distance in
the understanding of their own habits so that they would be
enabled to evaluate critically in the light of their basic
principles which of these habits should be retained, and
which could be transformed or discarded. He urged that
culture should be viewed as a pattern of habitual responses
inculcated in childhood. An effort would have to be made
to overcome this early conditioning so that persons could

think dispassionately about what really was good, instead
of merely affirming automatically traditional patterns of
thought and behaviour. It was necessary to open a debate
about cultural practices and to use reason to evaluate
habits. People should learn to ask whether specific
cultural practices were rationally justifiable.[13]

Sayyid Ahmad Khan has written that his personal search
for meaning resulted in the conviction that reason must be
trusted:

> Then I reflected that the tenet of the Muslim's
> faith, 'confession is by the tongue and
> affirmation by the heart' . . . is no doubt a
> true proposition. . . . I concluded that faith
> (iman) cannot be without certainty (yaqin) and
> certainty cannot be without knowledge (ilm).
>
> I also reflected that knowledge or certainty,
> without which faith cannot be acquired, must be
> like the certainty about ten being more than
> three, so that its truth is enduring. Because
> if it were not, it would not be true knowledge
> or certainty--it would be nothing but delusion.
> . . .
>
> Then I asked myself how reason can with
> certainty remain free from error. I admitted
> that such certainty is not really obtainable.
> Only if reason is used constantly can the error
> of the reason of one person be corrected by the
> reason of a second person and the reasonings of
> one period by the reasonings of a second.[14]

Sayyid Ahmad Khan's warning to his people that they must
begin to think dispassionately about their beliefs and
practices was thus founded on his personal conviction that
no one ought to accept beliefs and practices which could
not be justified by reason. If one could not justify one's
belief, then affirmation by the heart would not be
possible, and the belief would be little more than a habit.
He recognized that justification of beliefs and practices
was necessary and also that no justification could be
final, since the reasons given were always potentially
capable of being proved wrong by other persons, or by
future generations. This dilemma led him to the conclusion
that one could only do the best one could by way of seeking
valid reasons. One must remain open to the ideas of others
so that the on-going process by which the members of the

community as a whole test their convictions might continue.

Sayyid Ahmad Khan's sense of the transcendence of God
allowed him to view human efforts to attain certainty as
ultimately inadequate, because final certainty was with
God alone. He noted on his travels on the boat to England
the diversity of human religious practices: "I saw the way
God was prayed to, and admired His catholicity. Some men
bow down to idols; others address Him seated on chairs,
with heads uncovered; some worship Him with head covered
and beads on, with hands clasped in profound respect; many
abuse Him, but He cares nought for this. He is indeed the
only One who is possessed of the attribute of
catholicity."[15]

From Sayyid Ahmad Khan's perspective, God was not
partisan in many of the conflicts between humans; human
notions of appropriate behaviour were often limited by many
finite concerns. Many of these concerns were remote from
the transcendent goodness of God himself. God required
humans to recognize that transcendent goodness existed
outside and beyond the capacities of their finite minds.
His goodness accepted all finite attempts to express
gratitude and homage. Nothing human was foreign to God,
but He was transcendent to, and aware of, all.

The Qur'an and Nature

Sayyid Ahmad Khan was severely criticized both during
his lifetime and subsequently for his emphasis on nature as
a criterion for evaluating religious belief and practice.
He was condemned by many as a naturalist (nechari). Those
making the condemnation seemed to think that he was somehow
reducing religious seriousness to a matter of this-worldly
concerns, rather than of awe before the reality that was
outside and beyond this world. The criticism arose partly
because he criticized traditional beliefs in angels and
miracles as irrational. The very call to self-criticism
which he placed before his community was perceived by many
as an insulting attack based on foreign values.

Yet he was not the first to urge Indian Muslims to

reform their beliefs and practices. A reform movement,
comparable in certain respects to the Reformation in
Christianity had been taking place in many parts of the
Muslim world for some time. The Indian manifestation of
this movement was sometimes called the Wahabi or Mujahidin
movement. It had certain similarities to comparable groups
in the Arab world, but it was an indigenous Indian
movement. These reformers had preached that Muslims should
uphold the unity of God against all shirk (anything other
than God). The classical term shirk refers to the sin of
associating anything else with God. In this case, it meant
idolatrous and innovative practices. The reformers claimed
that they wished to restore pure Islam, to purge Indian
Muslim practices of foreign accretions, such as distaste
for widow remarriage, prostration at the feet of alleged
holy men, reverence for tombs, elaborate religious
festivals, and the exaltation of divine power in Muslim
heros such as Hassan and Husain.

Sayyid Ahmad Khan was sympathetic to many aspects of
this reforming movement. His family had blood connections
with some leaders of the movement, and they had supported
the reformers' activities. He had written about its
leaders in his study of the religious personalities of
Delhi, and had even referred to himself on occasion as a
Wahabi. He shared the concern to revive an Islam purified
from medieval beliefs and practices that had no
legitimation in the Qur'an or in the early practices of the
Muslims. He differed from the Wahabis more with repect to
means than to ends. They tended to dislike rationality,
and to demand immediate action. One of their leaders had
written:

> He alone who reposes his sole reliance on
> God, and does not pursue any other
> course, is liked by Him, and is guided in
> the right path; thereby he derives that
> comfort and ease of mind which never
> falls to the freethinker . . . the whole
> career of the life of a rationalist is
> nothing but misery and distress; while
> that of the other is incessant comfort
> and happiness.[16]

The author of these lines ended up killed in a battle,

which was part of a holy war, _jihad_, which he and his
associates had undertaken against the Sikh rulers of the
Punjab. Their notion of "trust in God alone" carried with
it the implication that the believers were simple
instruments of his will who should cast themselves on his
mercy, as it were, and fling themselves into battle for his
cause.

Sayyid Ahmad Khan was fourteen when that battle
occurred. He was certainly well aware of the point of view
that led those reformers into what some conceived of as
glorious martyrdom. His own rationality may be seen in
part as a rejection of puritanical extremism as an
effective instrument of reform. He rejected the hope for
incessant comfort and happiness that might have come from
casting his life into a battle conceived of as the will of
God. He chose instead the more awkward and emotionally
less comforting path of sustained thinking. He did not
believe that intense emotional commitment was proof that
one knew the will of God for a specific situation.

Sayyid Ahmad Khan had turned to a study of classical
Muslim theology and philosophy for guidance. The
understanding of nature he found there may be indicated by
the following quotation from Ibn Miskiwaih:

> Nature is simultaneously the totality of
> material beings and the law that governs
> their motion, the active force that
> energizes them to growth and perfection.
> Nature is not material nor is it a
> function of matter. It is the lowest of
> all spiritual existence, the slumbering
> Soul, so to say.[17]

Although Sayyid Ahmad Khan, in accepting the conclusions of
the astronomy of his age, necessarily rejected the
hierarchical cosmos which underlay earlier world views such
as this, he yet thought of nature, especially in ethical
matters, in a manner very similar to many of those among
his predecessors who had been concerned with ethical
thinking. He, too, thought of nature in terms of
potentiality, and this potentiality existed also in human
mind and character. He saw this potentiality of nature as
evidence of the goodness of God.

Sayyid Ahmad Khan also found nature to be a concept
widely used among the European thinkers of his age. He was
particularly attracted to the views of Thomas Carlyle
because that author had refuted the centuries of Western
condemnation of Muhammad by arguing that the original
success of Islam had been based on its naturalness. In his
preface to his own study of the Prophet Muhammad, Sayyid
Ahmad Khan quoted Carlyle. The Muslim's signature, which
comes right after the quotation, has the effect of a
profound "Amen":

> 'A false man found a religion: Why, a false man
> cannot build a brick house: If he do not know
> and follow truly the properties of mortar, burnt
> clay, and whatever else he works in, it is no
> house that he makes, but a rubbish heap. . . . A
> man must conform to Nature's laws, be verily in
> communion with Nature and the truth of things,
> or Nature will answer him. . . . It is like a
> forged bank note; they get it passed out of
> their worthless hands; others, not they, have to
> smart for it. Nature bursts up in fire-flames,
> French revolutions, and such like, proclaiming
> with terrible veracity that forged notes are
> forged.'
>
> Syed Ahmed[18]

Sayyid Ahmad Khan's signature at this point seems to
indicate not only that he was grateful to Carlyle for
vindication of the Prophet's honesty, but also that Sayyid
Ahmad, too, understood that during the on-going historical
process falsehood eventually would be consumed by the
"natural" reactions of the oppressed or mistreated. Sayyid
Ahmad Khan had experienced the chaos of the Indian Mutiny,
whereas Carlyle had studied the French Revolution. Both
had concluded that folly on many sides had resulted in
disaster.

Nature had thus connotations for Sayyid Ahmad Khan of
the innate potentialities of individuals, and also of the
inherent characteristics of social institutions. An
unnatural form of social organization would not long endure
because natural forces themselves would erupt and overthrow
it. He saw little conflict between the Qur'an and nature
as he understood it. In fact, he believed that the Qur'an
taught that individuals had potentialities which could be

realized and that corrupt societies would not long endure.

At one point in his essays on the life of Muhammad,
Sayyid Ahmad Khan presented a list of Qur'anic teachings.
These were:

> Set up not up another God with the True God,
> lest thou sit down in disgrace and destitute
> (17.23).

> Thy Lord hath commanded that ye worship
> none besides Him, and that ye show kindness
> unto your parents, whether one of them or
> both of them attain to old age with thee.
> Therefore say not unto them, Fie on you,
> neither reproach them, but speak
> respectfully unto them (17.44).

> And submit to behave humbly towards them
> out of tender affection, and say O Lord have
> mercy on them both, say they nursed me when
> I was little (17.25).

> And give unto him who is of kin to you,
> his due, and also unto the poor and the
> travellers, and waste not thy substance
> profusely (17.28).

> And let not thy hand be tied up to thy
> neck, neither open it with an unbounded
> expansion, lest thou become worthy of
> reprehension and be reduced to poverty
> (17.31).

> Kill not your children for fear of being
> reduced to wrath; we will provide for them
> and for you. Verily killing them is a
> great sin (17.33).

> Draw not near unto fornication, for it is
> wickedness and an evil way (17.34).

> Neither slay the soul which God hath
> forbidden you to slay, unless for a just
> cause (17.35).

> And meddle not with the substance of the
> orphan, unless it be to improve it, until he
> attain his age of strength, and perform your
> covenant, for the performance of your
> covenant shall be inquired into hereafter
> (17.36).

> And give full measure when you measure
> aught; and weigh with a just balance; this
> will be better (17.37).

> And follow not that whereof thou hast no
> knowledge, for the hearing, the sight, and
> the heart, every one of them shall be
> examined at the last day (17.38).
>
> Walk not proudly in the land, for thou
> canst not cleave the earth, neither shalt
> thou equal the mountains in stature. All
> this is evil and abominable in the sight of
> thy Lord (17.39.40).
>
> These precepts are part of the wisdom
> which thy Lord hath revealed unto thee. Set
> not up any other God equal unto God lest
> thou be cast in to hell, reproved and
> rejected (17.41).[19]

A good Muslim must thus be God-fearing, kind,
respectful, humble, generous, thrifty, optimistic, chaste,
just, responsible, law-abiding, accurate, meek, and
iconoclastic. Fear and hope are the traditional attitudes
inculcated by Muslims: a pious person is to live by walking
the delicate line of harmonious balance--the straight path,
sirat-al-mustaqim. He must neither fall into the arrogance
of autonomous pride (failure to fear the final justice of
God) nor the folly of despair and disbelief (failure to
trust the goodness and mercy of God). Sayyid Ahmad Khan
remained a traditionally pious person in the sense that
his conviction about the importance of reason did not
invalidate his recognition of the finitude of human
efforts.

The Prophet Muhammad is normally understood by Muslims
to represent the highest virtues because he was the man
entrusted to deliver God's revelation, and to lead the
people in their efforts to work out the implications of
that revelation in their political, social, and economic
institutions. Sayyid Ahmad Khan envisaged the Prophet's
virtues thus:

> The Prophet of God was extremely beautiful
> and attractive. . . . His face shone
> brighter than the moon on the fourteenth
> day of the month. His body was neither
> fat nor really lean but rather of middle
> size. When you saw him from afar he would
> appear in perfect beauty and comeliness
> and sweetness. . . .
> His beauty was enhanced by his utter
> moral goodness, he was not angry ever, nor

revengeful, except when God's rights were
at issue. He was courageous and most
generous especially with the poor and with
travellers; yet regarding his own needs he
was parsimonious. He showed modesty in
his conduct, was forbearing and humble and
free from envy and lust.
    In short, 'Whoever saw him for the first
time would be filled in his heart with
reverence and awe whilst a person
permanently in his service would be filled
with utmost affection and love for him.'[20]

This utter moral goodness exemplified by the Prophet
is the highest ethical ideal for Sayyid Ahmad Khan. The
Qur'an, as he understands it, teaches the virtues that make
such goodness possible and warns against the vices that
militate against the development of such qualities of
character.

Public Morality--Jihad and Ijtihad

Jihad is the term commonly translated as holy war,
whereas ijtihad is the technical term used to refer to the
intellectual effort made on questions of jurisprudence.
Both come from the same root, which means to endeavour, to
strive, to take pains. The puritanical reformers referred
to earlier were sometimes called Mujahidin, or persons
committed to fighting a holy war, jihad. The question of
whether the Indian Muslims of Sayyid Ahmad Khan's day ought
to plunge into a jihad against the British was a live issue
in mid-nineteenth-century India.[21]

An Englishman, W. W. Hunter, had written a book
entitled The Indian Musulmanes, Are They Bound in
Conscience to Rebel Against the Queen? The author thought
that rebellion was being preached throughout India as being
incumbent on Muslims and that Muslims were susceptible to
such teaching. Sayyid Ahmad Khan thought that British
prejudice against the potential rebelliousness of Muslims
was dangerous for his community because if the British saw
his people as rebels, they would repress them. He wrote a
review in which he attempted to refute the charges. His
position was that jihad was not incumbent on Muslims when
the government under which they were living allowed them

religious liberty. Further, he said that the original
jihad in the first Islamic century had been a matter of
self-defence. The subsequent wars fought by Muslims were
only wars, but not jihad. A true jihad was very rare and
would not be characterized by cruelty or mercenary ends.[22]

Sayyid Ahmad Khan maintained that the religious
precedent for Muslims to accept living under foreign rule
was the Qur'anic narrative of Joseph in Egypt. The
political tensions of the nineteenth century were, as he
saw them, a matter of political dispute only. Religion
ought not to involve itself with these conflicts:
"Moreover it should be borne in mind that the wars of the
present day . . . cannot be taken as wars of religions or
crusades, because they are not undertaken with religious
motives; but they are entirely based upon political matters
and have nothing to do with Islamic or religious wars.[23]

Sayyid Ahmad Khan was aware that medieval Muslim
history had included a great deal of fighting between
various groups. Muslims had sometimes fought other Muslims
or Hindus or Sikhs. Alliances had taken place among all
the various groups, depending on the exigencies of the
time. A Muslim invader from Afghanistan had ravaged Muslim
Delhi and carried off the Peacock Throne. Another Muslim
warrior had blinded an aged Muslim emperor. Sayyid Ahmad
Khan thought of wars like this as an aspect of the real
political world; they were not to be dignified by the label
of jihad. One should fight if necessary, but one should
not assume that one's political purposes were readily
identifiable with the will of God. Luther had urged
Christians to give up the notion of Crusades for a similar
reason.

Thus, Sayyid Ahmad Khan did not think that the
fighting during the 1857 Revolt, or in the other conflicts
in India, ought to be labelled jihad. He did not consider
that the Indian Muslims had a religious reason to fight
against the English, as long as they enjoyed freedom of
religion. He did not seem to expect that the original
jihad would necessarily ever be repeated.

Turning now to ijtihad, we note that Sayyid Ahmad Khan

was strongly of the opinion that all aspects of Muslim
religious law should be reconsidered. He shared the
nineteenth-century conviction that written legal codes
provided a better source of justice than unwritten custom.
If the codes were written, persons had a possibility of
complaining and having the laws changed. When unwritten
custom dominated, possibility for change was remote and
difficult. He also believed in the value of constitutional
government, and he saw this type of government as a vast
improvement over earlier forms of tyranny.[24] Despotism was
despotism, whether the despots were Muslims or others. He
saw the new understanding of the possibilities of changes
in government and law as liberating for all the citizens.
Those who feared the new and who wanted to return to
despotism were foolish and naive in his view. He did not
have a romantic idea of the virtues of the Indian Muslim
past.

The opposite of ijtihad is taqlid, submission to
authority. In urging Muslims to accept new forms of
education and scientific training, Sayyid Ahmad Khan was
exhorting them to abandon traditional notions of authority
in all areas of life. Rationalism meant that all ideas had
to be tested and debated. With reference to religious law,
this meant that the Qur'an, the hadith, and the shari'a
should be discussed. In terms of the Qur'an, commentaries
should be written that would indicate what all the
different points of view had been and were, with respect to
the meaning of particular verses. When the individual
considered these various meanings, he or she should be free
to choose for himself or herself whatever meaning seemed
satisfying.[25] Membership in the community should not be
dependent on selecting any one interpretation over others.

Sayyid Ahmad Khan was very critical of the use of
hadith as a source of religious law because he considered
that much of the material contained in these traditions was
unreliable. He would not accept using hadith as a basis
for interpreting the Qur'an. He wanted a review of these
materials that would sort them out again in the light of
modern critical methods. The basic principle should be

conformity with the Qur'an; hadith that went against the
Qur'an should not be accepted as authoritative. Further,
hadith would have to satisfy standards of rationality if
they were to be acceptable as exemplary.[26]

In his view, the unchanging element in human
religiousness was the aspect of personal relation with God.
Sayyid Ahmad Khan used the word din for this personal
religiousness, as contrasted with shari'a, the social and
political aspects of the religious tradition. He said that
these latter aspects necessarily changed as the conditions
of life in the world changed. Therefore, Muslims should
not seek religious guidance on matters of clothes, housing
and general conditions of life. These changed with the
times and were not central to religion.[27]

He knew that the Western hostility towards Islam was
often based on the writings of western scholars like
William Muir, who had written a life of Muhammad. Muir and
others had used hadith materials as a basis for their
descriptions of Muslim beliefs and practices. Sayyid Ahmad
Khan was concerned to deny that these hadith materials
truly represented Muslim life as it had been or should be.
Much of it he considered forged and unreliable. He gave
the following dignified reply to Muir's assertion that in
Islam "freedom of judgment in religion is crushed and
annihilated": "With respect to Islam, it can be safely and
confidently asserted that its nature is diametrically
opposed to the remark of Sir Wm. Muir, and that, perhaps,
there is no religion upon earth superior to it in respect
of the liberty of judgment which it grants in matters of
religious faith."[28]

Muslims were thus persons free to interpret for
themselves what God required of them. The Qur'an was
addressed to each person and should be internalized by that
person. The social, economic, and political affairs of the
community should be dealt with by institutions in which all
members participated. Problems should be handled by
rational methods. Matters such as usury or punishment of
criminal behaviour should be dealt with by the courts
according to procedures and standards deemed just and

reasonable by the citizens. Standards of earlier ages need
not necessarily apply. Just as slavery was an institution
that had been accepted by earlier ages, which was now
discarded, so also other practices might be discontinued
if the community agreed. The criterion was the opinion of
the citizens based on rational discussion. With respect to
theology and legal thinking, Sayyid Ahmad Khan thought that
the medieval treatises were filled with minutiae, sometimes
with far-fetched expositions and absurd reasonings.[29]
Therefore, all the legal and theological thinking would
have to be done over again so that fallacious assumptions
and defective logic might be discarded. Although he
offered his own opinion on most of the central issues, his
main point was that the method of rational and
dispassionate discussion should be followed. He was more
concerned to indicate how social and political and economic
matters were to be handled than to impose final solutions.

He pointed out that in the classical hadith not even
one-twentieth of the materials dealt with administrative
matters.[30] The rest was concerned with matters of ritual
and exemplary materials related to personal religious life.
This meant that the understanding that administration
should be handled on the basis of reason was traditional.
The difference in the modern period was that it was now
possible to involve more of the citizens in the decision-
making processes.

Sayyid Ahmad Khan also held something like a theory of
voluntary associations. He did not expect the state to be
the main agent in implementing reform. Rather, he
advocated self-help as a basic virtue.[31] In his own
lifetime, he organized and participated in a number of
voluntary associations concerned with translation
activities, educational reform, and the dispersion of
scientific ideas. His educational reforms came about
through his own efforts in soliciting funds and setting up
the new college for Muslim students. On matters of this
kind, he wanted the Muslims on their own to undertake all
the activities necessary to change the way their children
were educated. This meant that he did not want reforms

imposed arbitrarily on people who did not want or
understand them; persuasion was central to his view of
effective human relationships. Those who wanted change had
the obligation to persuade rationally their fellow
believers of the validity of their ideas.

The transformation of society should come about
through the free co-operative efforts of citizens. A basic
principle of his social thought was that the problems would
differ from age to age. The solutions of one age would not
be adequate for another. For this reason, the process of
social criticism was on-going. Reform should always be
taking place because institutions would never be perfect.
Self-help meant that citizens should continually be
challenged towards the solving of common problems through
co-operative action. The function of religion in this
co-operative society was to inculcate the values of justice
and mercy that would lead to the formation of sensitive
consciences in individuals. When such individuals grew up
having internalized awareness of the need to strive for
justice and mercy in human relationships, they would have
the necessary basis for working constructively together to
make their patterns of common life good. In a recent study
of the basic themes of the Qur'an, Fazlur Rahman has
indicated that this "sensitive conscience" is the principle
virtue proclaimed by the Qur'an.

> This unique balance of integrative moral action
> is what the Qur'an terms taqwa, perhaps the
> most important single term in the Qur'an. . . .
> Hence, taqwa means to protect oneself against
> the harmful or evil consequences of one's
> conduct. . . . This idea can be effectively
> conveyed by the term 'conscience', if the
> object of conscience transcends it. This is
> why it is proper to say that 'conscience' is
> truly as central to Islam as love is to
> Christianity when one speaks of the human
> response to the ultimate reality--which
> therefore, is conceived in Islam as merciful
> justice rather than fatherhood.[32]

Sayyid Ahmad Khan's understanding of rationality in
the exercise of ijtihad carried with it this kind of notion
of the trustworthiness ultimately of Muslim consciences.
Muslims could be trusted to judge wisely in the exercise of

their rights to rethink the legal bases of their common
life because they carried in their inner beings a sensitive
awareness of the characteristics of righteousness. The
ethical thinkers of the Islamic tradition almost always say
that one should never act or make a decision while angry.
One cannot think clearly or evaluate honestly while one is
emotionally upset. Hence, the rationality of the good
judge, or political thinker, or ethicist, is close to the
clearness of mind of the good scientist or historian. The
conscience does not operate well when the vision is
obscured by clouds of rage or jealousy. The training of a
sensitive conscience is a matter of great skill and
discipline. It must begin in the young child, but it is
continued throughout life through the medium of friends and
family. A devout life of worship is necessary to it so
that the awareness of transcendent standards is maintained.

An example of Sayyid Ahmad Khan's own moral reasoning
can be found in a speech he delivered while introducing a
bill to make vaccination compulsory in the Northern
Provinces of India, as a member of the Vice-regal
Legislative Council from 1878 to 1882. During that period
he supported a bill on compulsory vaccination. In his
speech on that subject, he acknowledged that he did not
approve of the state compelling citizens against their
wills to change their customs.

"No one can hold stronger views than I do, that no
measure relating to the welfare of the public should be
adopted by the State without due regard to the feelings
of those to whom the measure relates."[33]

Nevertheless, he maintained that compulsory
vaccination was necessary because of the thousands of
innocent children suffering from the disease. He believed
that the state should persuade through education, and that
officials should be responsive to citizens. The state
should rarely enforce measures which the citizens did not
understand or approve.

Purdah, Crime, and Sin

Some of his admirers have thought Sayyid Ahmad Khan to
have been too conservative with respect to women. He
condemned those Western critics who accused Muslims of
mistreating their women, but he also hesitated against
advising Muslims to change too quickly their patterns of
marriage and family life. In arguing against Western
critics, he said that Islam had given more rights to women
than other religious traditions. Muslim women had the same
rights as men in relation to their ultimate
responsibilities as individuals freely responsive to God.
They had rights over their own property and the freedom to
make their own decisions about marriage.[34]

However, in an article entitled Purdah, Sayyid Ahmad
Khan said that change should not be made just because of
fashion.[35] He was clearly worried about the dangers of too
rapid social change in this matter and inclined to feel
that the limits established by the shari'a should be
respected. Some of his biographers have noted that the
women of his own family had achieved a high level of
personal culture within the Purdah system. He felt that in
number of respects Muslim insights into relations between
the sexes were superior. For example, the permission to
divorce was wiser than Christian absolutism. Sayyid Ahmad
Khan said that Western thinkers such as Milton and Luther
were moving closer to Islam when they advocated divorce.
He thought that many of Luther's reforms indicated an
"islamicizing" of Christianity.[36] He knew that polygamy
was one of the customs for which Muslims were most harshly
criticized by Europeans. He said that the classical Muslim
view of polygamy was more balanced than the Hebrew Bible,
which permitted unrestricted polygamy, or the Persians,
who had no rules as to which relationships were
permissible, or the Christians, who looked on marriage as a
sin and who advocated celibacy as the ideal. He quoted two
Qur'anic verses: "But if you fear that you shall not be
able to deal justly, then have only one (wife)" (Qur'an
4:129). "Men are never able to be fair and just as between
women even if it is their ardent desire" (Qur'an 4:129).[37]

The traditionalist manner of handling these two verses is to acknowledge that the first gives legal permission, even though the second indicates that ideally a just relationship would not be feasible. Sayyid Ahmad Khan and other liberal reformers have urged that the second verse should take priority as representative of the ideal. The position of the liberals is that the processes of history have made the implementation of the ideal more feasible. Just as the abolition of slavery was an ideal not capable of being realized in the early Islamic centuries, but subsequently realizable, so also monogamy should be recommended now that it was practicable.

Sayyid Ahmad Khan favoured the education of women, although he did not want girls to be educated away from their homes. For boys, however, he preferred a residential community for them away from home, in which they would learn to overcome superstitious attitudes and develop self-discipline. They should learn a sense of common purpose so that Muslims from all over India might develop mutual sympathy among themselves and prepare themselves for the co-operative work of the future. The girls, however, needed to be prepared for the more traditional responsibilities of home and children. But Sayyid Ahmad Khan also said that when the men had become more educated, they would know how to look after the rights and educational needs of their women.[38]

With respect to usury, Sayyid Ahmad Khan quoted this verse: "They who return (to usury) shall be given over to the fire" (Qur'an 2:275). His view was that exegesis of scripture involved a consideration of its intention with respect to the context at the time of revelation. He argued that the original intent of this verse was to prevent the exploitation of poor people who could not pay and who were being grievously mistreated by their creditors. The crime, as he saw it, lay in the mistreatment of persons for the poverty which they could not help. They should have been constructively helped. But he saw no harm in charging interest to persons who could afford to pay it. He said that when loans are

arranged in such a way that the community as a whole
flourishes, then good has been done.[39]

On the issue of the cutting off of the hands of the
thief, he discusses the following Qur'anic verses:

> And as for the thief, whether man or woman,
> cut off their hands in recompense for their
> deeds (Qur'an 5:38).

> Only, the punishment of those who war
> against God and His prophet and who strive
> to make mischief in the land, is alternate
> hands and feet should be cut off or they
> should be banished from the land (Qur'an
> 5:33).

In interpreting these verses, Sayyid Ahmad Khan followed
the reasoning attributed to Abu Hanifa, the founder of the
school of law followed by most Muslims in the subcontinent.
The argument runs as follows: (1) In the second verse,
there is a choice between two types of punishment, hand
cutting or imprisonment. (2) In all the schools of law,
there is stipulation as to which goods would require the
hand cutting if they were stolen. This means that the
jurists did not consider the simple stealing of anything to
deserve this punishment. (3) There is good evidence that
even at the time of the Companions of the Prophet hands
were not cut off and only imprisonment was used.[40]

In sum, then, hand cutting is a possible form of
punishment, but not the only one. As indicated above, the
jurists had discussed issues of this kind exhaustively and
had attempted to arrive at solutions which would incorporate
as effectively as possible their grasp of justice. The
Muslim jurists of the past had often taken a long time
working through a process of mutual consultation to arrive
at conclusions. Sayyid Ahmad Khan was himself a person
whose professional life was spent dealing with legal
problems. There he was intimately familiar with the slow
procedures necessary for sifting evidence and for thinking
as comprehensively as possible about the implications of
decisions. His mental habits were those of a jurist.

On the question of the validity of using stoning as a
punishment for adultery, Sayyid Ahmad Khan followed the
earlier Indian reformer Shah Waliullah (1703-63) in arguing

that the practice did not receive its validation from the
Qur'an. He argued that its origins were in the Jewish
tradition and that it had been incorporated into Islamic
practices from that outside source. It was a practice
characteristic of a more primitive form of society and
should not be used under the changed conditions of the
modern world. In his opinion, the Qur'an was more in
harmony with modern attitudes because it did not advocate
stoning. Sayyid Ahmad Khan's method in handling these
Qur'anic teachings indicates that he considered that
decisions with regard to punishments for particular crimes
should be taken only after careful and rational discussion.
The Qur'an was to stimulate awareness of ideal human
potentialities, but the humans themselves had the
responsibility to work out, guided by reason, how to
implement in an effective manner the Qur'anic wisdom into
the structures of organized society.

Akhlaq connotes for Sayyid Ahmad Khan, as it did for
the earlier ethicist Ibn Miskiwaih, training individuals to
relate in a constructive way to other individuals. Ibn
Miskiwaih had emphasized the need to train persons to
relate to each other in an harmonious manner. As a
cultured member of a governing elite, he was well aware
that prosperity and stability in society demanded that
people learn to live in peace with others. The opposite
would be lawlessness and social chaos, a political reality
never too far distant from the horizons of medieval Islamic
societies. He believed that Islam had provided special
institutions to train persons to recognize their
obligations to brotherhood and sharing.

Sayyid Ahmad Khan, as another member of the cultured
governing elite many centuries later, had a very similar
view of the necessity of training persons to co-exist
harmoniously. Social discord was a reality he had
experienced in Bijnore during the 1857 Revolt. In
addition, the history of his city of Delhi in the hundred
years before him had been one of tumult and disorder. The
possibility of disruption and violence was extremely real
in that milieu, not only against Muslims from Hindus, Sikhs

or English, but among Muslims themselves. Hence, one had
to strive for an ordered society, but one could not take
for granted that it would exist. Like Ibn Mishiwaih,
Sayyid Ahmad Khan considered that Islam required training
believers to work together and to develop relationships of
sympathy and mutual support. He wrote:

> If you will reflect on the principles of
> religion, you will see the reason why
> our Prophet ordered all the dwellers in
> one neighbourhood to meet five times a
> day for prayers in the mosque, and why
> the whole town had to meet together on
> Fridays in the city mosque, and in Eid
> all the people had to assemble. . . . It
> is necessary for the good training and
> education of Mohammedans that they
> should be collected together in one
> place to receive it; thus, that they may
> live together and eat together and learn
> to love one another.[41]

Part of this training in attitudes which should lead
to social harmony involved an active effort to achieve good
relations with non-Muslims as well. Sayyid Ahmad Khan said
that the kind of reforming efforts which pictured members
of the other communities as evil tended to worsen
relationships. For example, he said that the forming on
the Hindu side of societies to prevent cow-killing had the
effect of stirring up more Muslims to kill cows.[42] Thus,
even to agitate against what the others were doing caused
them to do more of it and made the whole situation worse.
These pro and contra cow-killing agitations were part of
the increasing communal tensions of his time. His ethical
position was that one should never define oneself as
virtuous over against members of another group--a group
perceived as a manifestation of evil.

Sayyid Ahmad Khan encouraged Hindu students to attend
the college he had founded; he himself offered a reward for
the top Hindu student. The first graduate was a Hindu. In
Sayyid Ahmad's view, tolerance was not simply a passive
acceptance of persons from other communities; it was linked
with basic notions of human potentialities and of
rationality. It was possible and necessary to communicate
with other persons; one could discuss matters reasonably
with them and come to common conclusions. Hence, problems

could be solved by rational discourse. A society of
persuasion and mutual respect was the opposite of one
founded on violence and aggression. It was necessary to
reach out to other people, to learn their languages where
necessary, to adapt to their customs if advisable, and to
speak to them in such a way that they could hear and
respond. Sayyid Ahmad Khan's lifelong effort to encourage
communication between the Indians and the English sprang
from his belief in the common humanity that made persuasion
possible.

Sin is not a Muslim ethical term, nor is it a word
used by Sayyid Ahmad Khan. Nevertheless, in considering
the ethical stance of a writer, it is helpful to know what
is considered the antithesis of good behaviour. It is
evident from Sayyid Ahmad Khan's writings that bigotry is
the characteristic that he finds most reprehensible.[43] The
bigotry of the English was the worst obstacle to the
successful ushering of the Indian Muslims into the
prosperity of an industrialized society. The bigotry of
the Muslims was similarly the main obstacle to the
successful coping with their many urgent difficulties. The
bigot is a sinner because he is so wrapped up in
self-satisfaction and self-absorption that data from the
real world cannot impinge upon him. Like the philosopher
in Plato's story who earns the derisive mockery of an
observant servant girl when he falls in a well because of
his involvement with abstraction, Sayyid Ahmad Khan's bigot
is deaf, dumb, and blind to the real people and real
problems confronting him.

The wickedness of bigotry is clear from reason and
from revelation. The bigot is incapable of valid reasoning
because he cannot take seriously the arguments of other
persons and will not permit criticism of his own position.
The dispassionate analysis of the effective scientist,
historian, or ethicist is beyond his capacity since the
data cannot impinge on him. He is wrapped up in himself
and thus obsessed with his autonomy.

Autonomy and pride are characteristics roundly
condemned by the Qur'an. The virtuous person in Qur'anic

terms is open to astonishment before the reality of the
world around him; he sees "signs" of God's reality
everywhere and anywhere: "whether you look to the East or
the West, there is the face of God" (Qur'an 2.109). He is
not puffed up nor self-satisfied. He in not malicious, nor
jealous, nor gossip-ridden. He is just and ready to
forgive. He does not harbour vindictiveness.

> Perform the prayer, and
> bid unto honour, and forbid dishonour.
> And bear patiently whatever may befall
> thee; surely that is true constancy.
> Turn not thy cheek away from men in
> scorn, and walk not in the earth exultantly;
> God loves not any man proud and boastful.
> Be modest in thy walk, and lower thy voice;
> the most hideous of voices is the ass's.
>   (Qur'an 31.16)

This ass with the loud voice, in Sayyid Ahmad Khan's terms,
is the sinner; the ass's bigoted rejection of the reality
of other persons and his turning away from them in scorn
cuts him off from the possibility of genuine response and
co-operative life.

Sayyid Ahmad Khan's life was open and public. After
his wife died, he did not marry again, but rather spent the
last thirty-seven years of his life studying, writing,
fund-raising, organizing, and publishing. He was
continually in the midst of friends and co-workers. The
Muslim community as a whole was well aware of him and his
activities since he did so much active campaigning. Thus,
his ethical teachings could be recognized in the example of
his own life. His conviction of the universality of the
human capacity to be open to persuasion was indicated to
his fellow Muslims in his debates with the English. His
open criticism of the English failures in the pre-Mutiny
period helped convince Muslims that persuasion rather than
violence was a viable option for settling disputes.

The tributes paid to him indicate something of the
impact he had on his people. The Muslim historian, K. A.
Nizami, has summed up his influence: "He thus became a
social and moral force which accelerated the processes of
transition from the medieval to the modern age."[44] During
a presentation to him from the Indian association of Lahore

on the occasion of his visit to that city, the speaker
said: "Not the least remarkable feature of your public
career has been the breadth of your views and your liberal
attitude towards sections of the community other than your
co-religionists. Your conduct throughout has been
stainless of bias or bigotry."[45] And, finally, Sir Thomas
Arnold, an Englishman who had come to teach history at the
college established by Sayyid Ahmad Khan, paid this tribute
to his friend: "A nobler life, more void of self-seeking,
more devoted to truth, to the service of others, it has
never been my privilege to come in contact with. Where
shall we find one like him?"[46]

Abul Ala Mawdudi (1903-1979):
Islamic Fundamentalist

Abul Ala Mawdudi began his career as a religious journalist
in the period immediately after World War I when Indians
from many different backgrounds were becoming excited and
active in the struggle to expel the British from India and
to achieve self-government. He participated in the
Khilafat Movement, the agitation in support of the Turkish
Caliph, which was led by Muslim activists in the immediate
postwar period. The hope at that time was to preserve the
Caliphate as a safeguard for Muslim rights. But Gandhi
called off the non-co-operation movement after the violence
at Chauri Chaura. Since the non-co-operation movement and
the Khilafat movement were closely linked, the latter
collapsed after the Turkish revolution. This was a crisis
for the Indian Muslims because it left them with little
hope of help from Muslim power outside India. The leaders
reacted in various ways: some went over to the Congress to
work for a secular India; some abandoned politics
altogether and concentrated on education; some stayed with
the Muslim League as an alternative to the Congress.
      Mawdudi's own response was gradual. His background
was not that of the elite of the political leaders of the
Muslim League, most of whom had been educated at the
college founded by Sayyid Ahmad Khan. Mawdudi's father had
been taken out of Aligarh by his father, because the latter
feared the corruption of too much foreign influence.
Mawdudi had been educated privately at home by tutors. He
had not received the traditional religious education of the
members of the ulama class, nor did he take to wearing a
beard and exhibiting the external characteristics of that
group until later in his life. He was essentially a
self-educated person associated with no particular
discipline or school of thought. His initial responses
were highly individual. His first profession was as a
journalist and editor of the journal of the Indian ulama.

He began to attract notice with the publication of two
books, al Jihad fil Islam (1926) and Towards Understanding
Islam (1930). The latter book became so well-known that
it was prescribed as a text in schools. Mawdudi's
subsequent fame and influence derived in large measure from
the vigour and persuasive power of his writings.

In 1932, he took over the editorship of the monthly
journal Tarjuman al-Qur'an and continued in that role for
the rest of his life. He described the objectives of the
journal as the invitation to others to the truth which he
had discovered through his study of the Holy Book and the
Prophet's sunna. He said that his early understanding of
his traditional religion had proved inadequate for him; he
had had to devote himself personally to study in order to
discover the true system. Once he was satisfied that he
had found the truth, he set out to invite others to share
his discovery with him. Many of the articles first
published in the journal were later issued as books.

In 1941, he founded an organization entitled the Jama'
at-i-Islami. The group edits and publishes journals and
books. Its members organize welfare activities and
political action. There were seventy-five persons present
at the first conference of the Jama'at in 1941. In his
speech on that occasion, Mawdudi explained that persons
would not be accepted as members merely because they
professed to be Muslims; individuals would have to
demonstrate that they understood the meaning of Islam and
its requirements in a manner acceptable to the
organization. In other words, the organization would
certify who qualified as a valid Muslim; to have been born
and brought up a Muslim was not enough.

Mawdudi stood up and announced that he had renewed his
faith and had entered the Jama'at-i-Islami. The other
members were similarly expected to stand up and affirm that
they had renewed their faith. A Constitution was
established for the Jama'at. An Amir (leader) was to be
elected. When Mawdudi was chosen, the members pledged
their loyalty to him. He then selected a Majlis-i-Shura
(consultative council). The members were expected to

reform their own lives and to invite others to recognize
the sovereignty of God. They had to abstain from
professions dealing in interest, alcohol, dance and music,
gambling, bribery, etc. They could not serve any
government which did not accept the Qur'an and the sunna
as the source of laws. The party's structure was to be
pyramidal, and the Amir was the final arbiter of all
affairs, both organizational and ideological.[1]

Mawdudi opposed the Muslim League as well as the
Congress. His position was that the Westernized leaders of
these groups suffered from a slave mentality in their
adoption of Western attitudes; they would betray the true
interests of the Muslims. After partition, however,
Mawdudi and many of his followers went to Pakistan. One
part of the organization remained in India and has
continued to operate there. In Pakistan, he and his
followers have opposed all the subsequent governments as
being insufficiently Islamic. The regime of Zia al Haqq
has been the only exception. Mawdudi has served
occasionally as a member of some of the committees of
religious experts that the various governments have
convened to advise on religious matters. He has also been
imprisoned in 1948, 1952, and in 1964. Each time he was
considered a threat to public order because of the
virulence of his attacks on the alleged infidelity of the
political leaders. Members of his organization have been
candidates in various elections but have not had notable
success.

He continued to publish many books throughout this
period. His writings have been influential in many parts
of the Muslim world. His original book, al-Jihad fil
Islam, is said to have influenced Hasan al Banna, the
founder of the Muslim Brotherhood in Egypt. Several
leaders of that organization were imprisoned and killed by
Abd al Nasir after an attempt on his life.[2] However,
others continue to write, to recruit new members, and to
agitate against all leaders whom they consider betrayers
of the true Islamic system.

Mawdudi's insistence on the need for trustworthy

leadership is related to his original dissatisfaction with
the traditional scholar-jurists, and the liberal
followers of Sayyid Ahmad Khan and graduates of Aligarh.
His emotional stance is one of a person consciously alone
and appalled by the possibilities of forces of
disintegration, which he discerns all around him. He
perceives Western civilization as hostile to, and
destructive of, all the values that he affirms. Hence, his
situation is understood to be that of a representative of
the forces of truth and goodness, which are perceived as
threatened. The reply to the threat is to organize, to
find the faithful, to train them, and to persist. One must
work to restore the truth by recreating, in the face of
ignorance and hatred, the only good and true way for humans
to live.

The despair that served to arouse his will was great,
as was the effort to overcome the despair by firm action.
His will led to a vigorous life of writing books, editing
and publishing his journal, recruiting and training
followers, and taking part in what political activities
seemed feasible. He was willing to live simply and to
endure repeated jail sentences in the service of his ideal.
He represents to his followers a stirring example of
single-minded devotion.

Mawdudi's unity of purpose has carried with it an
emphasis on the necessity of authoritarian control. A
recent study of the activities of the Jama'at-i-Islami
indicates the effective control that Mawdudi has exercised
over the members of the group.

> Organisationally, Mawdudi's hold over the Jama'at
> rested on the system of whole time workers who
> were paid their wages from the treasury. In
> 1965, every fifteenth member was a paid worker.
> The leadership and its management was entirely
> under the control of these paid workers. It
> required great courage to differ from the Amir,
> when one's livelihood depended on one's agreement
> with the Jama'at. This fact assumes added
> significance when it is also considered that
> Mawdudi himself was the major source of the
> Jama'at's finances through his writings and
> publications while he himself was not dependent
> upon the treasury. He met his own expenses from
> some of his publications the royalties of which

he kept for his own use. . . . Naturally, a
leader of the party, who held the purse strings
and also had the right to interpret the Shariah
and whose Majlis-i-Shura (consultative body) was
bound by Constitution to yield to him, was bound
to have an unassailable position within the
organisation.[3]

The Ethical Viewpoint of Islam

Mawdudi's book The Ethical Viewpoint of Islam is a
vigorous statement of the position that underlies all his
writings. His aim is to persuade Muslims to a new vision
of their traditional religion. His way of doing this is to
attempt to convince them that the ethical teachings of that
heritage, properly understood, contain the only feasible
solution to the oppressive dilemmas of existence in the
modern world. The ethical viewpoint, in other words, holds
the key to all problems, to the transformation of
individual and social life, ahd to the rebirth of dynamic
Islam.

His rhetorical style is that of diagnosis, bringing
the patient to a recognition of disease, followed by
directions for the cure. He begins with an analysis of the
corruption of the modern world, as he saw it in 1944 when
this statement was made. He uses a metaphor indicating
that the stream of life is polluted by hidden filth, and
that in times of flood (crisis) all the rottenness at the
bottom is cast up. The foul realities under the smooth
surface of modern life are thrown up in the crisis of the
period.

Thus the moral vices, which the greatest part
of humanity was nurturing within itself for
ages, now stand fully exposed before us. . .
. Only the stark blind can now harbour the
delusion that all is well with the diseased
humanity. . . .
We see whole nations exhibiting, on a huge
scale, the worst morals which the conscience
of humanity has alway condemned with one
voice. . . . Every nation, by its own free
choice, selects its worst criminals and
places them at the helm of its affairs. . . .
There is no form of villainy . . . which
these nations have not been guilty of, on a
huge scale and with the utmost shamelessness,

> under the direction of their leaders. . . .
> Justice with these fiends means only justice
> for their own people. . . .
>   On a closer examination of the matter it
> would be found that ethically the body of
> humanity has become completely putrified. . . .
>   It is obvious that collective vices make
> their appearance only when individual vices
> have reached their nadir. . . .Therefore, if
> the peoples of the world are exhibiting on a
> large scale the seamy side of human nature
> through their collective institutions, that
> can only lead us to conclude that, in spite of
> all its intellectual and cultural progress,
> mankind is passing through a period of intense
> moral decadence which grips by far the
> greatest majority of human beings. If this
> state of affairs continues a little longer the
> time is not far when humanity will meet with a
> colossal disaster, and long ages of darkness
> will supervene.[4]

From such a perspective, only a radical transformation can
halt the onset of destruction. Hence, conversion to the
ethical viewpoint of Islam is required. This viewpoint
will be the antithesis of all that has been described
above. It will serve to purify humanity from all this
accumulated rottenness and will lay the basis for a perfect
and universal social order.

The method of Mawdudi's rhetorical style is to proceed
from the description of the disease to a consideration of
all possible medicines. The fallacies of the other
medicines are pointed out, and the conclusion is that only
one mode of cure can possibly work. The medicines
considered are the "moral and ethical concepts of the
world." All of these are invalidated. They include
polytheism, false other-worldliness, false emphasis on the
personal rather than the social in monotheism, and atheism.
None of these will work. They either fail to convince
humans to take the world seriously or they do not give a
strong reason for people to combat their own evil
tendencies. Ethical humanism will never work because it
gives insufficient motive for the reformation of
character.[5] Mawdudi explains the only cure:

> It is high time now that we should look about
> for a satisfactory basis of moral life. This
> kind of search is by no means a logical
> hair-splitting, but a practical necessity of
> life. . . .

The conclusion to which I have been led is
that there is only one correct basis for
morality and that basis is supplied by Islam.
Here we get an answer to all the basic
ethical questions and the answer is free from
the defects noticeable in philosophic replies
and untainted by other religious creeds which
create neither firmness and integrity of
character nor prepare man to shoulder the
immense responsibilities of civilized life.
Here we find a moral guidance which can lead
us to the highest virtue in every department
of life. Here we do find ethical principles
on which the edifice of a truly righteous
civilization can be raised and which, if
taken as the basis of individual and communal
conduct, can save human life from the anarchy
which has overtaken it to-day.[6]

A fundamental underlying principle of Islam as
presented by Mawdudi is theistic subjectivism; this view is
similar in certain respects to the perspective of the
medieval Asharites. Mawdudi finds the existence of many
and divergent points of view to be the source of evil and
chaos in society. If only one point of view dominates,
order and harmony will follow. This one point of view must
be that of God, since he alone could be accepted as the
authority capable of transforming all human wills into the
harmony of his will. If, he argues, you live on an estate
that actually belongs to another person, and you know that
you are his agent, you also know that he is the one to
decide what the rules are for looking after the estate.
Therefore, man's function is to submit himself to the
guidance of his creator, and to look after the well-being
of the world on the creator's behalf. Man is not to make
decisions himself regarding the badness or goodness of the
rules.

Man's status in the universe having thus been
determined, it follows logically that he has
no right to lay down the law of his conduct
and decide the right and wrong of it. This
is a function which properly belongs to God.
Once this is accepted, all ethical questions
which have been agitating philosophers since
ages past find easy solutions which are so
definite that they leave no scope for those
deep and widespread differences of thought
which have forced different sections of
humanity to follow widely divergent paths,
resulting in social conflict, moral chaos,

and intellectual disunity. . . . The real
sanction for morality is the fear of God and
the proper motive which ought to impel us in
observing the canons of morality and
abstaining from immoral conduct should be
love of God, the desire to seek His pleasure
and the fear of His displeasure.[7]

The Qur'an and the Sunna

In 1943, Mawdudi began publishing his commentary on
the Qur'an, Tafhim al Quran. One of his followers has
characterized as follows the impact of this commentary on
those who have responded to it:

It is a unique commentary of its kind and lays
. . . forth the true message of the Quran as a
revolutionary concept that God has sent for
transforming the entire human life. The
Tafhim throbs with life and dynamism and
expounds how the Quran wants to revolutionise
human society to establish the supremacy of
God in all walks of life on this earth. It
sets one thinking. It spurs one to get up
and do his duty. It fills man with a
dedicated spirit to perform his mission.[8]

This quotation indicates that Mawdudi has been
successful with many Muslims in persuading them to his
interpretation of the Qur'an. His teaching has been
essentially the same throughout his long career. The same
author notes that to many young Pakistanis of his
generation, the Sixties, the very word "Islam" suggested
the ideas of Mawdudi.

Mawdudi is not just a person he is an institution,
rather a movement himself. . . . The moment one
thinks of Islam in the present era, Mawdudi
invariably comes before the mental eyes. . . .
Most opponents . . . cannot extricate themselves
from the peculiar situation of propounding the
very same thoughts which Mawdudi has been
inculcating from decades and which have now become
part and parcel of everyone's subconscious. This
is the victory of Mawdudi. Malign him as much as
you can, throw him in jails and prepare even
gallows for him, but he rules over the hearts.
There is no excape from him.[9]

Although this praise comes from a supporter, it
nevertheless reflects in some measure the attractiveness
of Mawdudi's views for many of his fellow Muslims. He has

been extremely effective in the art of persuasion. This
effectiveness is in part a result of his ability to
convince his hearers that his teaching derives from the
Qur'an and the sunna. He has found there, he maintains,
answers to all the pressing dilemmas of modern existence.
In one of his articles, he sums up some of the Qur'anic
verses that seem most significant to him. These are:

> (a) And do not eat one another's property among
> yourselves, nor seek by it to gain the nearness
> of the judges that you may sinfully consume a
> portion of other men's goods and that knowingly
> (Qur'an 2:188).

> (b) If one of you deposits a thing on trust
> with another, let him who is trusted
> (faithfully) deliver his trust, and let him fear
> God, his Lord (Qur'an 2:283).

> (c) He who misappropriates (the public money)
> will come on the Day of Judgment with what he
> has misappropriated; then shall everyone be
> given in full what he earned (Qur'an 3:161).

> (d) The thief, male or female, cut off his or
> her hands (Qur'an 3:161).

> (e) Those who devour the property of orphans,
> unjustly, devour fire in their bellies, and will
> soon endure a blazing fire (Qur'an 4:10).

> (f) Woe to the defrauders who, when they take
> the measure from men, exact full measure, but
> when they measure or weigh for them, give less
> than is due (Qur'an 53:1-3).

> (g) Those who love that indecent things should
> spread among the believers for them is a painful
> chastisement, in the life of this world and the
> hereafter (Qur'an 24:19).

> (h) Force not your slave-girls to prostitution
> that you may enjoy (some gain of) the present
> life, if they desire to live in chastity. And
> approach not fornication, surely it is a
> shameful deed and evil way. The adulterer and
> the adultress, flog each of them with a hundred
> stripes (Qur'an 24:33).

> (i) O ye believers, wine and gambling and idols
> and divining arrows are an abomination--of
> Satan's handiwork; so avoid them that you may
> prosper (Qur'an 17:32).

> (j) God has permitted trade and forbidden usury
> (Qur'an 17:32).[10]

Mawdudi has concluded from these verses that God has
prohibited certain ways of acquiring wealth, namely, taking
others' properties by false pretensions, bribes, fraud,
theft, indecent activities, idolatry, and usury. Muslims
are commanded, he argues, to earn their living in
non-harmful ways, and not to love wealth exorbitantly.
Whatever is left over from their earnings after they have
cared for their families should go to charity. Mawdudi
says that the state has certain responsibilities in the
area of economic justice, such as collecting the poor tax,
zakat, and distributing it. But, in general, the state
should not interfere in economic matters: "It seeks to
enforce the other items in this plan through the
intellectual and moral uplift of the individuals comprising
a society and its general amelioration. Economic justice
is thus secured in perfect accord with the principle of
allowing the exercise of individual freedom in the economic
field."[11]

Mawdudi tends to think of economics in the modern
world by analogy with the trading activities of the first
Muslim community. Since business flourished in the
commercial world of early Islam, when the believers were
constrained only to give some of their profit to the
central authorities for the relief of the poor, he thinks
that trade and commerce can flourish in any age if a
similar pattern is followed. It is characteristic of his
approach that he does not see any need to deal differently
with economic questions because of changes in modes of
production and business organization. In his vision of
the ideal Muslim society, the same essential conditions
remain. Sayyid Ahmad Khan, by contrast, thought that real
changes had taken place, and that usury, for example, meant
something quite different in the commercial transactions of
industrialized society than it had meant in early Arabia.
Mawdudi, however, insisted that usury was still forbidden.
Whatever a creditor charges from his debtor over his
principal is unlawful, and God does not allow it as truly
earned income like the profit earned in trade.

Mawdudi argues that the command to pay compulsory

alms, _zakat_, is for the spiritual benefit of the believers:

> Zakat is not only for the good of society; it
> is also necessary for the moral development
> and edification of the giver himself. It is
> for his own purification and salvation. It
> is not only a tax but also an act of worship
> just like prayer. It is an essential part of
> that programme which the Qur'an prescribes
> for the amelioration of man's soul. . . . But
> the Qur'an was not content to infuse a
> general spirit of voluntary benevolence and
> philanthropy among people. It instructed
> the Prophet as the Head of the Islamic State
> to fix an obligatory minimum for it, and
> arrange for its regular receipt and
> disbursement.[12]

Mawdudi insisted against socialists and communists that
economic problems could be solved not by state control of
the economy, but rather by implementation of the overall
scheme of life based on the ethical concepts of Islam.

The Prophet symbolizes to Mawdudi the person who
successfully implemented a way of life in which all
problems were readily overcome. He believes that it was
possible for the Prophet and his followers to solve their
difficulties because they had responded fully and
faithfully to the revelation that had come to them in the
Qur'an. Their conversion and their faithfulness enabled
them to become persons who could deal effectively with the
economic and other problems of everyday life. The
conversion of hearts brought ready solutions to formerly
insoluble problems.

The political aspect of this overall scheme of life is
founded, according to Mawdudi, on the sovereignty of God.

> According to the Qur'an, the commandments of
> God and the Prophet of Islam constitute the
> Supreme Law and the Muslims as such cannot
> adopt any attitude other than that of
> complete submission to it. A Muslim is not
> allowed to follow his own independent
> decisions in matters which have been finally
> and unequivocally decided by God and His
> Apostle. To do that is a negation of
> faith.[13]

The most essential requirement for the implementing of a
society based on the will of God is the selection of men in
authority; they must be chosen on the basis of moral
excellence alone: "It is an ideological State which must

be run only by those who accept its basic ideology."[14]
Those who live in the state but do not accept the ideology
enjoy the same civil liberties as other inhabitants as long
as they agree to behave as law-abiding citizens. Citizens
have rights to be consulted, to develop their
personalities, and to protection from interference by
others. They are bound to a definite code of morality that
makes it obligatory to obey the orders of the State, whose
leaders are working in accordance with the laws of God, and
obligatory to co-operate wholeheartedly with the state in
the cause of virtue.

The Qur'an thus gives the blueprint for the ideal
human society. The Prophet was the man who had the
appropriate character and understanding to receive this
revelation, to appropriate it, and to implement it. One
well-trained by the Prophet, such as the Caliph Umar, would
similarly understand and implement this vision. Mawdudi
explains that the Prophet trained the Companions in a
manner that imposed hardships upon them and developed their
capacities for selfless service.

The Prophet's character was such that he "attracted
everyone by sincere godliness and absolute selflessness--
. . . free from all personal, family tribal and
nationalistic motives . . . people were convinced that this
was humanity at its best."[15] The result of his leadership
was a bloodless revolution that changed the mental and
moral outlook of the people.

Mawdudi insists that the word <u>din</u> means a way of life
and a rule of conduct. He vigorously opposes the notion
brought forward in the Turkey of Ataturk, and supported by
Sayyid Ahmad Khan and other liberals, that <u>din</u> meant
personal religiousness. The notion that religiousness
should be personal, whereas political and social matters
should be determined by unguided reason, is anathema to
Mawdudi. That it is wrong is demonstrated both by reason
and revelation. Reason tells us that humans need a system.
Without a system, Mawdudi finds it obvious that humans will
fall into chaos and disorder. It is self-evident to him
that corruption and evil would be the only conceivable

products of unfettered human wills. Revelation, as he
understands it, makes the same point.

Sayyid Ahmad Khan and other liberals used the Qur'anic
narrative relating to Joseph in Egypt to indicate that a
Muslim could be a devout and God-fearing religious person
while serving under a political system not based on
revelation. Mawdudi considers this interpretation entirely
wrong.[16]

Mawdudi often uses the metaphor of seeds and trees to
indicate his understanding of natural processes. Thus, a
mango tree cannot be grown from a lemon seed. This example
is used to explain why the righteous must flourish and the
wicked decay. A society based on the principle that
individuals were autonomous, subject to no will other than
their own, would come to destruction. A good tree cannot
be grown from a bad seed. A good society must be rooted in
sound principles, and these are the fundamentals of Islam.

In his book A Short History of the Revivalist Movement
in Islam, Mawdudi explains that the history of Islam is
different from the history of Muslims. Islam, understood
as the perfect human system, existed during the lifetime of
the Prophet and the first four Caliphs. Then the ideal was
replaced by kingship enforced by arms. The Muslim
societies that have existed since that time have not lived
up to the ideal. Hence, the duty of Mawdudi's generation
is to recreate the original, righteous Islam. This not
only ought to happen, but it inevitably will. Mawdudi says
that his aim is "to scientifically prove that Islam is
eventually to emerge as the World-Religion to cure Man of
all his maladies."[17]

The revolution that is to bring about the restoration
of true Islam must begin in the hearts of believers who
will commit themselves to struggling for the implementation
of divine will. They must build up their movement and then
seize power. They must establish the Islamic system of
life and arrange for the proper conduct of a society.
Mawdudi says that it is meaningless to believe in a system
unless one commits oneself to struggling to achieve the
power to implement it.

In sum, then, Mawdudi does not envisage conflict
between the Qur'an and nature. He does not see a split
between truths given by revelation and those apprehended by
reason. The Qur'an, nature, and reason all give the same
message according to his system of thought. Those who have
properly understood the Qur'an are the same people who
properly understand both nature and reason. The source of
corruption is the human will. A corrupt will cannot
apprehend revelation, nor comprehend nature, nor reason
effectively. The conversion of the will is an essential
first step to the development of the mind and the spirit.
Only those who can demonstrate their "right thinking" by
their readiness to commit themselves to Islam can be
considered to have a valid understanding of nature.

Mawdudi's commentary on the Qur'an shows that, in his
view, there is usually only one right way to understand the
various strands of Qur'anic thought. Sayyid Ahmad Khan had
said that interpretation of the Qur'an should explain to
people what the various interpretations had been with
respect to controversial matters and should give individual
Muslims the freedom to accept whatever interpretation they
preferred. A comparison of Mawdudi's commentary with that
of a scholar from the al-Azhar university in Cairo (one of
the major centres of Islamic theology) indicates a
significant difference of approach.[18] The latter
commentary gives the reader an analysis of the various
interpretations of particular verses that have arisen over
the long course of Muslim history. It does not insist that
only one view is valid for all Muslims. Mawdudi, by
contrast, only very occasionally indicates that a variety
of views have existed, or are possible. He rather explains
regularly and systematically just how every aspect of the
Qur'an is to be understood. This means in the end, of
course, that his readers necessarily apprehend the Qur'an
through his mind only.

Jihad and Ijtihad

Mawdudi's first book Al Jihad fil Islam was written to
defend Muslims against Hindu charges of fanaticism after
the murder of a prominent Hindu leader by a Muslim zealot
in 1926. Throughout his subsequent writings, Mawdudi
continues to view Jihad, understood as the struggle to
implement the truth, as an essential facet of a devout
Muslim's duty. Mawdudi maintains that the nature of piety
requires a serious religious person to be prepared to offer
himself in the service of divine will.

In his commentaries on Surahs 8 and 9, two parts of
the Qur'an dealing with jihad, he tells believers:

> Muslims do not go to war for the sake of
> material gains but for the sake of
> reforming the moral and social evils in
> the world in accordance with the
> principles of truth.[19]

This notion of challenging the whole world is implicit in
Mawdudi's understanding of Islam, because all that is not
Islam is for him unbelief, kufr. The basic religious model
for Mawdudi is thus that as a person comes to understand
the reality of God's will, he must offer his whole being
and life in the service of that will. Those who refuse to
acknowledge the reality of God are guilty of kufr. The
root of this word means to be ungrateful. Kufr is
equivalent to infidelity, godlessness, ingratitude. In
religious terms, ungratefulness lies in failing to
acknowledge the goodness and reality of the Creator from
whom all life derives; this failure separates the
unbeliever from truth. The system of faith in Mawdudi's
understanding is a matter of either/or. To be inside means
total commitment; to be outside means total failure. Those
inside must never allow the outsiders to dominate or to
exercise influence, because if this were to happen the will
of God would be frustrated: "Jihad applies to all those
efforts that are made to degrade the world of Kufr and to
exalt the Word of Allah . . . in the initial stage or by
fighting in the final stage of the struggle."[20]

Mawdudi's mind is dominated by the paradigm of the
successful Prophet.[21] All of human history is understood

by him to be explicable in the light of this paradigm. The
urgent necessity for the present situation is to repeat the
paradigm. In the beginning, a successful revolution
occurred because the Prophet and his Companions responded
faithfully to revelation and implemented a perfect society.
The same success will inevitably occur if the present-day
believers will have an equivalent power of faith. Jihad
in this context means the total commitment to struggle for
the forces of light against the forces of darkness.

This position is essentially a-historical in the sense
that nothing new is considered to happen in history. The
vast pageant of the historical process is conceived of in
the light of this one conflict only. The light has been
manifested only in the brief period of the Prophet and the
early Companions; all else, including all of Muslim
history, has been darkness. Mawdudi's call to jihad is a
demand that the light be restored to a dark world. The
light can be restored only by those persons who have, as it
were, conquered the darkness in themselves, who have become
purified so that they might be instruments of the divine
power.

Mawdudi himself thinks in many ways like a modern man.
For example, the idea referred to above that "Islam is to
emerge as the World-Religion to cure Man of all his
maladies" indicates a modern cast of mind. This statement
suggests that Mawdudi conceives of divine will as immanent
in a historical process which inevitably leads to a
particular end. Those who understand that divine will are
the interpreters and instruments of the process. In this
respect, the God who makes known right and wrong is working
through history to a particular end. Only those who
comprehend this process are able to make true moral
judgments. The divine is conceived of here as an immanent
will to revolution. One aspect of the relationship between
Mawdudi's conception of the basic paradigm--that the pious
implement a successful revolution--and theistic
subjectivism is that Muslims must not question the
paradigm. In other words, believers must accept the
necessity of serving the Islamic revolution and of

following the leaders of that revolution. Their service
might take any form, depending on the actual situations in
which they found themselves. It might mean literal
fighting, but that is only one of many possibilities. They
must, however, be committed to a common struggle toward one
end.

The ideal Muslim character, as exemplified by those
who were accepted as full members of the Jama'at-i-Islami,
was marked above all by the virtues of obedience and
faithfulness. Other persons were considered associates,
but relatively few were accepted as full members. These
had to be carefully screened. This notion of membership,
based on a close scrutiny of one's character and attitudes,
is new in Islam and owes more to the example of Western
sectarian groups than it does to the Islamic tradition,
which had always been notably open and catholic in
membership. In the medieval period, the only offence that
justified exclusion from the community was leadership of an
armed rebellion against the state. Apart from that,
membership was open to all who were born Muslim or who
professed themselves Muslims.

In Mawdudi's theory, only those screened in the proper
way would be competent to rule the Islamic state. There
would not be opposition parties in his state; appropriate
persons would inevitably rule justly and in accordance with
the will of God because of the righteousness of their
personalities. In actual practice, dissension occurred
several times within the Jama'at-i-Islami, but the
dissenters always had to leave.

"Whatever Allah wills, He fulfills it anyhow, and man
can never defeat His plan with his counter-plans nor
prevent it from happening nor change it in any way
whatever."[22] The notion that God's will is a plan, a
scheme, inevitably working itself out in the historical
process is a modern rather than a medieval idea. The
righteous leaders whom the organization trains are expected
to dominate the world inevitably because of the certainty
of the effectiveness of God's plan. Further, "The real
spirit of this state lies in subordinating politics to

morality."[23] The plan Mawdudi sees is that this ideal
state will be free from the bad "political" characteristics
of all other contemporary states and will be devoted
exclusively to inculcating and maintaining morality among
its citizens. This morality will be defined from above;
there will be no way for the citizens to avoid the
responsibility of obedience in fulfilling the moral
requirements of their leaders. The system of Jama'at-i-
Islami allows for consultation, but only within the
permitted framework.

Ijtihad in matters of the religious-legal code is
favoured by Mawdudi because he is not satisfied with the
legal structures elaborated by the medieval jurists. These
jurists, in his view, had participated in an imperfect
system because by their time the religious and political
authorities had, to a certain degree, become separated.
The political authorities after the death of Ali had not
attempted to receive recognition as authoritative
interpreters of the Qur'an and the sunna, or as persons
competent to deal with religious law. They ruled, but the
jurists handled the matters of interpreting the religion.
The founders of the main schools of Islamic law were often
in conflict with the political authorities of their times.
Some of them had to endure imprisonment for their views.
The majority of Muslims in the world belong to Sunni Islam,
which means that they have accepted as legitimate both the
legal structures worked out by these early jurists and the
implicit division of powers that occurred after the death
of Ali.

Mawdudi wants to restore the position that existed
before that division of powers and to unite religious and
political authority in one entity, the Amir and his
consultative council. In arguing this way, he says
something new; he attempts to reverse the decision made by
earlier Muslims to accept that division. Those trained in
traditional legal schools have believed that what the
consensus of legal scholars has decided cannot be reversed.
Mawdudi supports ijtihad because he wants to reverse even
that basic premise of medieval jurisprudence.

In the system he envisages, a parliament would not be permitted to legislate on the basis of human reasoning, except on those matters on which the shari'a is silent.[24] Here again the criterion for the ability to reason justly is the prior commitment of the individual. The person allowed to deduce from the laws is the one acceptable in terms of Mawdudi's characterization of a good Muslim, namely, one committed to his particular view of the nature of the Islamic revolution.

In practice, as the members of the Jama'at-i-Islami have had to take positions regarding actual problems in Pakistan, they have faced dilemmas. One striking difficulty arose when the members of the group had to decide whether or not to support the candidacy of a woman, Fatima Jinnah, to be President of Pakistan. Mawdudi's teachings had clearly stated that it was invalid for a woman to participate in active politics, or to be head of an Islamic state. Nevertheless, at the time of this election, it happened that Mawdudi was in jail. He had been put there by the person actually in power, the candidate opposing Jinnah, Field-Marshall Ayub Khan. Given the choice between a woman and a man so wicked that he had imprisoned Mawdudi, Mawdudi decided to support the female candidate. Instructions came from Mawdudi in prison that the members of his group should support her candidacy and work for her election. They did so, but she failed to win. Some dissension occurred within the group on this matter, and the dissenters had to leave. The change of position was justified by a theory of choosing the lesser of two evils.[25] The particularly significant fact, in terms of Mawdudi's understanding of ijtihad, is that he made that decision himself. The Amir has the authority to make decisions, as indeed Umar and the early Caliphs once had. Mawdudi does not like the idea of democracy based on the notion that the people are sovereign and have the right through their elected representatives to design laws and other social institutions as they wish.[26]

In reality, medieval rulers were often extremely arbitrary and dangerous despots, which is why Sayyid Ahmad

Khan was receptive to the notion of limiting arbitrary
power by constitutions and legal codes. Mawdudi seems to
think that the shari'a would serve to limit the arbitrary
power of modern despotism, even though it had not been
markedly effective in accomplishing that goal in medieval
Islam.

After the establishment of Pakistan, many debates have
taken place about the nature of the Islamic state. Mawdudi
has several times been a member of the committees of ulama
which various Pakistani governments have convened to offer
guidance on religious questions. The members of the ulama
class have had an ambivalent relationship with Mawdudi.
They have admired the vigour of his leadership, but have
not always been ready to accept his authority on all
matters. [27]

Purdah, Crime, and Sin

Mawdudi's book entitled Purdah and the Status of Woman
in Islam, written first in 1939 and re-issued in English in
1972, is a strong statement of the attitude to sexuality
and family life that is central to his ethical position.
His persuasiveness in this respect is perhaps linked to the
vividness with which he portrays the horrors of the
non-Islamic world. Christian missionaries who attacked
Islam in their preaching in the nineteenth and early
twentieth centuries often focussed on alleged mistreatment
of women as a reason why Muslims ought to abandon Islam for
a "higher" religion. Mawdudi explicitly inverts this
attack. He says that the matter of the veil, which has
been the main instrument of abuse against Islam, is
actually the great glory and honour of the Islamic system.

The introduction to the book Purdah and the Status of
Women in Islam quotes a report of a nudist wedding held in
Florida at which the bride wore only a veil and high-heeled
shoes. This incident is held up as proof of the
fulfillment of the Western movement to emancipate women and
men. "It suggests the virtual return of man to animality,
to wild life wholly bereft of shame and decency."[28]

From this perspective, the opposite of Islam is
unrestricted animal appetite. Mawdudi makes a leap from
the microcosm to the macrocosm in his understanding of
"human and decent" as opposed to "animal" nature. With
respect to the microcosm, he argues that the Qur'an teaches
that man has both an innately animal and a human nature.
The two are in conflict. The guidance of revelation is
required to strengthen the human so that it may overcome
and repress the animal. The same conflict exists on the
level of the macrocosm. In one social and political system
the animal aspect dominates; in the other, the guidance
leads to human decency.

In Mawdudi's view, "the sex instinct is the greatest
weakness of the human race."[29] Satan is dominating the
modern world because animality is everywhere in power and
is depriving women of feelings of modesty and shame. Islam
is the antithesis of depraved society: "It is only Islam
which can provide wholesome atmosphere for the development
of high morals and noble traits of character and which can
guarantee true progress of man's intellectual, spiritual
and physical abilities."[30] The aim of the good society is
to "prevent the sexual urge from running wild, to moderate
and regulate it in a system."[31]

The basis of the system Mawdudi recommends is, in his
terms, haya. He does not offer an English term because he
considers the notion too central to Islamic morality to be
translatable. He quotes hadith to this effect: "Every
religion has a morality, and the morality of Islam is
haya."[32] He interprets this to mean that the ideal human
attitude is the shyness that a person feels before his own
nature and before God. This shyness is the quality that
prevents man from indulging in indecency.

Mawdudi uses hadith as his authority very extensively
on several matters. Since the hadith books contain the
materials used by the community in developing guidance for
actual practice, they contain more details than the Qur'an
does. Mawdudi also refers repeatedly to the evidences from
nature that he believes support his interpretation of the
Qur'an. Thus he argues that nature has made the male

active and the female passive. From this it follows, in
his view, that for the female to attempt to be active would
be unnatural and wicked.

Mawdudi assumes that the workings of God's mind are
readily intelligible to the right-minded humans. He says
that God is an engineer who has designed the factory of
human life to function in a particular manner.

> The existence of both the active and the passive
> partners is equally important for the purposes
> of the Factory. . . . But the Engineer Who has
> designed these parts fits them in the machine in
> such a manner that both become equally endowed
> and honourable, yet dominant and yielding as
> required by their respective natures, so that
> they may fulfil the purposes of their
> sex-relation.[33]

Yet, in spite of the alleged naturalness of this
system, Mawdudi nevertheless says that people may have to
be terrified into accepting it. With respect to the
Qur'anic teaching that persons who commit fornication
should be punished with one hundred lashes, he argues that
this practice is essential for the well-being of the
community. "The Western people abhor the infliction of a
hundred lashes. This is not because they dislike the idea
of physical torture. It is because their moral sense has
not yet fully developed."[34]

A person with developed moral sense, in Mawdudi's
view, will understand the terrible consequences of
fornication for the whole society. He will think that the
severe punishment of a few is a proper price to pay for the
safeguarding of hundreds: "Once the Shari'ah punishment is
carried out, it so terrifies the whole population that no
one can dare commit it for years to come. In a way it
performs a psychological operation on the minds of those
having criminal tendencies, and this reforms them
automatically."[35]

The ideal Muslim society will thus be one in which
modesty is deeply inculcated. Women will not leave their
homes. They may acquire some degree of education which
will enable them to become more adequate wives and mothers,
but their lives must be spent within the house. The males
must practise their moral duties by protecting the females

of their family and by guarding themselves against sexual
impropriety of any kind. The well-being of the whole
society requires this discipline of family life.

With respect to fornication, there are two relevant
passages in the Qur'an. Four witnesses are required. In
one passage, punishment is discussed: "Such of your women
as commit indecency . . . detain them in their houses until
death takes them or God appoints for them a way" (Qur'an
4.19). Traditional Qur'an interpretation held that the
"way" in question was laid down by the subsequent
revelation in Surah 24.2: "The fornicatress and the
fornicator--scourge each one of them a hundred stripes."

Mawdudi comments on the process throughout the Qur'an
of abrogating certain verses by later ones.

> This gradual enforcement of criminal law was
> based on sound practical wisdom. At the
> time the Arabs were not accustomed to live
> under a settled government with a regular
> system of law and judiciary. Therefore it
> might have been unwise and too much for
> them, if the Islamic State had imposed on
> them its complete system of criminal law all
> at once. That is why at first the sort of
> punishment contained in these two verses was
> enforced and then gradually stricter
> punishments were prescribed for fornication,
> theft, slander, etc., and finally that
> complete system of law was evolved which was
> in force during the time of the holy Prophet
> and his rightly guided successors.[36]

Unlike the liberal Muslims who thought of some of the
Qur'an's ordinances, such as references to slavery and
flogging, for example, as having been conditioned by the
social conditions of the earlier age and as being,
therefore, not applicable to later ages, Mawdudi
characteristically insists that the complete system was set
up in its ideal form by the Prophet.

There is also another aspect of the fornication
question. With respect to slave girls, the Qur'an says:
"they shall be liable to half the chastisement of free
women" (4.30). The traditional understanding of this verse
had been that slave girls should receive fifty lashes over
a six-month period. The Kharijites had argued that this
verse meant that stoning for adultery, a punishment not

found in the Qur'an, but legitimated by <u>hadith</u>, was wrong
since half of the death penalty was not feasible. The
majority did not accept that view. Mawdudi argues that
this interpretation of the Kharijites is wrong because the
verse in question must be understood to refer to free
unmarried women rather than to married women. He considers
the adultery of a married woman to be much more serious,
deserving of the death penalty.

> It is obvious that an adulterous married free
> woman deserved capital punishment for this
> heinous crime because she enjoys the double
> protection of the family and of the husband
> and that punishment is 'stoning her to
> death'. Though the Qur'an does not
> explicitly mention punishment of stoning her
> to death, it does indicate it in a subtle
> manner, which the Holy Prophet understood and
> enforced.[37]

The phrase "it is obvious" at the beginning of this
quotation indicates that, for Mawdudi, the meaning of the
Qur'an is self-evident, even on a matter not mentioned by
the Qur'an. The implication seems to be that the adultery
of married women is so terrible a crime in Mawdudi's mind
that stoning seems obvious to him as the appropriate
punishment. The liberal interpretation on this matter
would argue that the stoning was an idea brought into later
Islam from outside, Biblical sources and that it was
contrary to the Qur'an. Mawdudi is reacting against this
type of reasoning in his insistence that the punishment was
intended by the Qur'an, even though it was not stated. In
traditional practice, the lashes and the stoning were
rarely lawfully imposed because of the extremely exacting
standard of proof required, and also because of the
principle that such punishments are averted by any
circumstances of doubt. Mawdudi makes the issue much more
fundamental to his notion of the Islamic system than it was
in the legal thinking of the many jurists who preceded him
in earlier times.[38]

The worst sin in Mawdudi's system of thought is <u>kufr</u>,
failure to acknowledge the validity of the system which he
believes to be God's plan for humanity. <u>Kufr</u> is both
individual and social. Individuals may fail to respond to

the truth; all the other human societies are founded on and
dominated by kufr. Given the paradigm of a revealed plan
for a social revolution, there can be no significant good
other than the subordinating of one's being to the purpose
of implementing the plan.

Those who, like Sayyid Ahmad Khan, say that other
communities have some grasp of wisdom and truth, and that
relationships of co-operation and good will are possible
between human beings from many different cultures are
putting forth a position that is explicitly anathema to
Mawdudi. Any statement in favour of foreign modes of
behaviour, whether in clothing or in matters of political
structures or anything else, is seen by Mawdudi to be a
sign of "slave mentality." Thus, the reforms advocated by
Sayyid Ahmad Khan, such as changing eating habits and
playing English games like cricket, were seen as a betrayal
and a selling out to the destroyer of Islam. Mawdudi's
father had been removed from Aligarh after a friend had
seen him playing cricket. Mawdudi thinks that response to
foreign culture must be either a selling out or a total
withdrawal from pollution. No middle path seems feasible.

He stresses that sexual depravity in the non-Muslim
societies is proof of the necessity of retaining the pure
Islamic system free from contamination by contact. Mawdudi
dwells on sexual sins to a degree unusual in Muslim ethical
thought. Sayyid Ahmad Khan was more a traditional Muslim
thinker in his emphasis on arrogance and vain boasting as
the major evils in human character. Traditional Muslim
thought has emphasized pride rather than sexuality as the
source of most human error and grief. But Mawdudi is
concerned with the threat of disintegration of Muslim
family life implicit in the new mores coming from outside
Islam. Hence, he emphasizes the danger to human well-being
of uncontrolled sexuality. The beast in humans is seen by
him to be near the surface, and ready to disrupt ordered
relations between the sexes.   He fears sexual licence.

In sum, the phrase, "the complete system of law which
was in force during the time of the Holy Prophet and his
rightly guided successors" is the key to Mawdudi's

understanding of Islamic ethics. As he understands the
position of Muslims in the mid-twentieth century, forces of
chaos and disintegration threaten ominously. The chaos of
uncontrolled sexuality is one fearsome threat, as is the
pressure from foreign values, and foreign power. Muslims
are in danger of losing their faith, their self-respect,
and their control over their lives. The forces of
destructive unbelief (kufr) are perceived as everywhere
present and aggressive.

Mawdudi's answer is to name the threats he perceives,
and to diminish the power of these threats by demonstrating
their sources, and by indicating how they can be overcome.
His description of the destructiveness of Western patterns
of life and thought is one instance of the "naming" of the
threats. The widespread appeal his writings have for many
Muslims stems in part from the clarity with which these
books describe the problem and explain the answer. He
tells his Muslim readers what causes the anxieties they
feel, and what they need do to find direction and relief.
His answers often do provide extensive relief because they
use the vocabulary of the tradition, and because they are
clear.

Ethics in this context means submission to the
"complete system of law". Morality means acceptance of
directions from the leaders who are trusted as guides to
the will of God. To be good is to obey. Those who choose
to submit to this direction believe that all human life
will become good once all other humans have similarly
submitted to the directions issued by these leaders.

Conclusion

> This modern man, as he undergoes the world-shattering
> movement from fate to choice, easily impresses one as a
> Promethean figure. Often enough, especially since the
> Enlightenment, he has so impressed himself. It is all the
> more important to see that he is a very nervous Prometheus.
> For the transition from fate to choice is experienced in a
> highly ambivalent manner. On the one hand, it is a great
> liberation; on the other hand, it is anxiety, alienation,
> even terror. . . . Liberation and alienation are
> inextricably connected reverse sides of the same coin of
> modernity.[1]

Peter Berger maintains that modernity is characterized
by ways of life that offer greater numbers of choices to
individuals. The changes brought about by technology
transform the consciousness of individuals. Persons become
more self-reliant, and more aware that they can, in many
respects, take their lives into their own hands. The
movement away from fate is a process of increased awareness
of possibilities of changing the conditions of life. But,
Berger says, this increase of freedom can, and often does,
result in an increase in feelings of loneliness and
meaninglessness. The support given by the unchanging
structures of older forms of social order disintegrate
gradually, and this leads to an increase of confusion and
loneliness. The values used to be more clear, and
authority was more readily accepted. The confused modern
person has more choices, but much less idea what he or she
ought to do, or even what would satisfy her, or make him
feel better. Berger says that these dilemmas arose
originally in the societies which were first
industrialized, but that they are now present everywhere as
technology spreads the changes in consciousness that are
inevitably characteristic of industrialized societies.

If we understand that liberation and alienation are
inseparably connected reverse sides of the same coin, we may
more easily see why the perspectives of Sayyid Ahmad Khan
and Mawdudi both emerge out of the changes in consciousness

that persons in the Muslim world, as elsewhere, are
undergoing. Berger also says that persons in any tradition
faced with these new forms of consciousness have three
possible responses: they can reject their traditional
values entirely, they can try to reassert unchanged
traditional values, or they can try to select and to use
affirmations from the past that can be meaningfully
appropriated for the present and the emerging future.[2] If
they take this third position, they have to struggle to
relate the past values to modern experience.

Berger is not discussing ethical stances, but I think
that his analysis can readily be used to help illume the
matters we discuss here. In using the notion of cumulative
tradition, I indicate the attitude he mentions as the third
possibility. From this standpoint, the concern is to
select from the storehouse of past perspectives, exemplars,
and ways of thinking that may be useful in dealing with the
present and the emerging future. To use Weberian
terminology, the selection in the cases of Sayyid Ahmad
Khan and Mawdudi is done in a charismatic rather than a
bureaucratic manner. In Muslim terms, taqlid is replaced
by ijtihad.

If we assume that moralities are languages of
persuasion, we then have to note that, in the case of
charismatic authority operating in a new situation like
that posed by modernity, the persuasiveness of the rhetoric
of the particular morality will depend on the
self-authenticating quality of the language. Persons will
agree or disagree because of individual responses to the
words, not merely or necessarily because the words are
legitimated by a traditional bureaucracy. Individuals also
respond differently to old words; some teaching from the
past may come alive again in quite a new way, serving
different purposes than it ever did before. The Muslim
philosopher-poet Muhammad Iqbal said that the Qur'an is a
catalyst to awaken persons to a wider sense of reality,[3]
exactly what I intend in suggesting that old words can
evoke new reactions. Modernity carries with it literacy
and the printing press. Muslims are now able to read the

Qur'an for themselves as they were not generally able to do
in earlier times. This fact in itself changes the
authority of those who used to be the sole interpreters of
the Qur'an. Now one finds instances of Muslims who testify
that reading the Qur'an for themselves has had an
electrifying effect on them. For example, Muhammad Ali
said: "This book . . . has had the invariable effect of
intoxicating us, with its simple grandeur, its intense
directness and its incessant flow of motive power for the
manifold activities of life."[4]

Iqbal also said that life moves with its past on its
back.[5] He was responding to the extreme changes in Muslim
life and thought initiated by the Turkish revolution of the
twenties. He maintained that these changes involved social
change that was too fast and too radical. He was well
aware that many changes would take place, but he wanted
Muslims to be able consciously to direct the alterations
that would occur in their lives. The image of moving with
the past on one's back is a suggestive insight into the
functioning of tradition.

Sayyid Ahmad Khan and Mawdudi both explicitly want to
move forward. Neither of them wants to return to the
structures of life in medieval Islam. Neither wants, as it
were, to turn the clock back to pre-modern ways of life.
One aspect of this forward-looking perspective is therefore
recognition that the bureaucratized authority structures of
the Middle Ages no longer operate as they used to do. In
medieval Islam, political rulers, who usually had achieved
their power by force, exercised almost total authority.
The scholar-jurists and the sufis operated within the
society in interaction with the political rulers and
administrators. Those who held power might, if they
wished, take advice from scholar-jurists and sufis, but
they could not be forced by restrictions other than those
they wished to acknowledge.

Muhammad Mujeeb, in his history of the Indian Muslims,
has shown that over the many centuries of Muslim rule in
India a great diversity of different forms of interaction
took place between rulers, administrators, scholar-jurists,

and sufis. The sufis in particular, but also some of the
scholar-jurists, were often extrememly wary of involvement
with the state; they knew that it is risky to give advice
to a despot who has absolute power. They often had to
choose between becoming the tool of the despot's purposes
and isolating themselves from the state, and in the process
accepting relative poverty. There is a long history within
Indian Islam of religious thinkers refusing to involve
themselves with the state.[6]

Thus, the movement away from the acceptance of
medieval forms of bureaucratized authority with respect to
ethical thinking can also mean a change from the situation
in which the religious thinker either had to support a
basically despotic power structure, or to opt out of any
concern for improving the conditions of life in the world.
Within the medieval context, the acceptance of taqlid
(adherence to authority) on matters of jurisprudence and
theology had been one way of ensuring a certain consistency
of pattern as a protection against despotic power.

We noted that a discontinuity occurs between medieval
and modern ways of thinking on ethical matters as authority
structures change. Muslims lost power in India with the
failure of the revolt of 1857. When that happened, there
were no longer Muslim rulers for scholar-jurists or sufis
to advise. In the century since, sufi orders have largely
ceased to operate. The scholar-jurists have reponded with
more vigour. A significant new training centre was founded
by and for them at the turn of the century, and they have
been finding new ways of operating, particularly as guides
and supports to people enduring the rigours of social
change.[7]

In spite of these changes, however, the political
control of the Muslim community in the Indo-Pakistan
subcontinent is in the hands of persons whose educational
background in modern universities makes them relatively
unsympathetic to advice from the scholar-jurists who have
not had similar intellectual training. There has,
therefore, been a shift in perception of who is competent
to give advice on ethical matters. Any given Muslim might

well ask advice from a scholar-jurist or a sufi, but he or
she might also read a book or a newspaper article. The
The fact that Sayyid Ahmad Khan and Mawdudi both tried to
communicate their visions through editing and writing for
journals, as well as by writing books, indicates that they
understood the necessity of new forms of communication. If
an individual derives his or her ethical thinking in some
measure from what he or she reads in a book, he or she is
exercising autonomy in ethical thinking. No-one else might
interpret that book in the same way, nor need any of the
individuals that person lives and works with necessarily
share the insights gained. The individual is thus allowed
by the circumstances to choose and to decide in a more
autonomous manner than had earlier been the case.

Sayyid Ahmad Khan and Mawdudi both considered ethical
thinking to be the most important instrument of social
change. Each perceived the members of his community to be
living in a crisis precipitated by contact with more
industrialized societies. The language they used thus not
only employed the standard rhetoric of their tradition, but
also sought to put new content into old modes of
expression. Each selected from the cumulative tradition of
Islamic ethical thinking models that he thought would serve
to direct the beliefs and practices of the Muslims into
more effective ways of dealing with their immediate
problems.

Within the Islamic context, the standardized
vocabulary would include, as it did in these two cases,
legitimation from the Qur'an, hadith, the jurists, the
theologians, the sufis, and the philosophers. This does
not mean that any one ethical thinker would use all these
sources, but rather that abundant material was available in
all these areas as part of the common heritage. The notion
of cumulative tradition means that a reservoir of materials
exists from which appropriate choices are made in the
context of particular situations. Any given ideal or model
might not have been in active use for some time, but it
still exists and can be brought again into active service.
Thus, objective rationalism in ethical thinking had been

less used after the twelfth century, but was revived in the
nineteenth.

This revival does not mean that the modern forms of
objective rationalism and theistic subjectivism are exactly
similar to the earlier positions. Those trained in the
madrassas have learned labels such as Mu'tazila, or
philosophy, or naturalism, and they tend to apply these
labels easily to any new phenomenon that appears to
resemble the schools of thought they have heard about. In
reality, however, exact repetition cannot occur because the
other aspects of the problem necessarily differ. For
example, we noted that Sayyid Ahmad Khan as a young man had
defended the classical Muslim theory of the relationship of
the sun to the earth, and that he changed his opinion on
this matter because the evidence offered by modern
astronomy seemed convincing to him. His rationality was
thus linked to his conviction that evidence would have to
be given for conclusions in every aspect of life. The
modern physical and social sciences shaped his
understanding of rationality. Although the earlier
Mu'tazila had wanted to use reason as the criterion for
establishing justice, they had not thought of societies as
continually changing. Sayyid Ahmad Khan's belief that the
process by which one age might correct the errors of an
earlier age was on-going would not have occurred to the
earlier Muslim rationalists. The difference lay in much
greater knowledge and sophistication about history. Sayyid
Ahmad Khan's rationality was therefore not identical with
the earlier rationalism of the Mu'tazila.

Similarly, Mawdudi's type of theistic subjectivism
differs from that of the Asharites because he, like Sayyid
Ahmad Khan, thinks of changing existing social conditions.
The medieval forms of theistic subjectivism tended to serve
to legitimate the status quo. The Asharite theologians
advocated an attitude of uncomprehending awe before the
unknowableness of the divine will. Thus, whatever happened
was right because human beings had no instruments to
evaluate the relative goodness of the given. Mawdudi's
system, however, is not at all supportive of a given order.

His group of righteous reformers believe that they do have
criteria to evaluate and to challenge the given. These
criteria are available to them because, as they see it, of
their own righteousness.

Sayyid Ahmad Khan and Mawdudi thus both want social
change and both seek models from the past to legitimate
their demands. But they differ seriously in their
understanding of the nature of the historical process.
Sayyid Ahmad Khan thought of history as an unfolding of
varying ways of implementing the orignial vision of the
community. From his perspective, one age succeeded
another, each one bringing its own challenges. There was
never exact repetition. Believers in each age should draw
on wisdom from their cumulative past, but they would have
to face new problems and make new decisions. Sayyid Ahmad
Khan argued that perfection was never achieved within
history.[8] Each generation should strive as best it could,
but it should never imagine that its solutions were perfect
or binding on future generations. The process rolled
inexorably on, and new difficulties would always be
forthcoming. One set of problems would be solved, but
another would arise.

Mawdudi did not envisage history in this way as a
cumulative process. He rather thought of the ideal and the
corrupt as static entities. The ideal had existed
perfectly once; the corrupt had overthrown the ideal; the
ideal must in turn overthrow the corrupt. There is no
recognition from this perspective of imperfection in
whatever might be achieved, or of a certain degree of value
in all systems. Because the imperative is to realize an
absolute, the demand on the believers is intense. They
have to expunge totally from themselves and their social
organization all traces of the impure. Mawdudi thus hoped
for a greater perfection than Sayyid Ahmad Khan ever did,
but he also had a much more pessimistic understanding of
actual people and the existing conditions of his own world.

Both these Muslim ethical thinkers legitimated their
understanding of human nature from the same Qur'anic
sources, but they interpreted the sources differently.

Both took the Qur'anic image of Adam as the representative
human being, created as a potential killer, yet trusted
with responsibility for the well-being of the universe, and
helped through guidance given by God. For both, therefore,
human beings were understood to have animal characteristics
that needed to be guided and directed by controls. The
optimism of one thinker as contrasted with the pessimism of
the other stems from a difference in interpretation of just
how bad this animality is, and where it lies. In the
Qur'an the angels tell God that man is a killer:

> And when thy Lord said to the angels,
> 'I am setting in the earth a viceroy.'
> They said, 'What, wilt Thou set therein one
> who will do corruption there, and shed blood, . . .
> He said, 'Assuredly I know
>   that you know not.'
>   (Qur'an 2.26)

In another passage, man's folly is indicated:

> Man prays for evil, as he prays for good;
>   man is ever hasty . . . .
> We never chastise, until We send forth
>   a Messenger.
>   (Qur'an 12.12)

The teaching is that God has revealed ways to overcome
folly and destructiveness. Sayyid Ahmad Khan understood
animality as a characteristic that could be restrained by
good training. He thought of sound Muslim moral training
as the educating of habits of self-control such as he had
received from his mother and from the cultural milieu of
Mughal Delhi. When he speaks of bad qualities, he refers
to jealousy, meanness, spite, and uncontrolled emotion.
The good Muslim should not be dominated by his emotional
responses. He should be trained to respond with justice
even to attacks on himself. Sound training should lead one
to internalize controls. A well-trained, hungry adult
would think first of the hunger of the others. His
educated humanity would control his animality.

Mawdudi, on the other hand, saw animality as a much
more pervasive and overwhelming problem. His insistence on
the necessity of a leader who could establish a
comprehensive system is an index of his lack of confidence
in Muslims as individuals with internalized controls. They
would have to be moulded into good persons by the system

which the leader and his group of carefully selected moral
companions would implement. Animality could only be
overcome by those adults who would stand up as his
followers had done and consciously renounce their earlier
errors and bad ways. Goodness was thus very difficult,
requiring an intense effort to change. Each adult must
reform and become a totally committed person. The bad were
all those who would neither make this commitment nor pledge
their existence to the implementing and maintaining of the
system. That which overcame animality was not rationality
and self-control, but the intensity of the emotional
commitment to the system.

This basic difference in their interpretation of the
significance of the Qur'anic imagery thus leads to and
sustains their distinctive attitudes to other Muslims and
to non-Muslims. Sayyid Ahmad Khan's understanding of
virtue meant that other persons were transcendent realities
and had to be taken seriously. Any one person's grasp of
truth stood always in need of correction from others;
serious attention had, therefore, to be paid to the others.
To comprehend the realities of a particular situation, such
as the 1857 Mutiny, one would have to overcome one's
emotional reactions and to view as objectively as possible
all the many diverse causes of the event.

Rationality in Sayyid Ahmad Khan's case meant that all
persons were potentially capable of overcoming their
emotional reactions, of disciplining their responses, and
of entering into a reasonable discussion about actual
situations. They were capable of reaching agreement about
the causes of difficulties and about practicable solutions.
Hence, his effort in writing his Causes of the Indian
Rebellion was to persuade the English that they had made
mistakes. His other volume on the Mutiny, The History of
the Bijnore Rebellion, indicates that he hoped to persuade
all concerned that the violence which had occurred had led
only to greater disorder. It had solved none of the
serious problems facing the Indians who had to relate to
the British dominance of their country. He said that when
violence developed, the dacoits (robbers) came out of the

jungle.[9]

Mawdudi's efforts at persuasion were not similarly
motivated by efforts to explain in careful detail the
causes and solutions of immediate problems. He rather had
one solution only which was intended as an answer to all
problems. Sayyid Ahmad Khan's persuasiveness was directed
to the mind; his readers were asked to calm down, to quell
their emotions, and to think clearly and systematically
about the actual reasons for their troubles. They were to
debate and discuss slowly. Mawdudi's hearers were rather
expected to respond with an increased commitment of the
will. Both writers were effectively persuasive with many
of their fellow citizens because they wrote vigorously and
well. But the persuasiveness was of a very different kind
inasmuch as one was an invitation to think, and the other a
call to repent and to join an exclusive group.

Sayyid Ahmad Khan appealed to rationality because of
his fundamental confidence in the potential reasonableness
of all human beings. Although he had experienced harsh
criticism from members of his own community, and arrogant
racism from certain of his English acquaintances, he
nevertheless remained confident that the obtuseness and
bigotry which abounded everywhere could yet be transcended.
His own openness won him friendly response from many
individuals of diverse backgrounds. He did eventually
succeed in establishing the educational system for young
Muslims that had been his greatest ambition.

Mawdudi had none of this confidence in the potential
reasonableness of human beings. This lack of confidence in
others is an essential characteristic of fundamentalism.
When the others cannot be trusted, when one's own
intuitions are the only reliable clues to fundamental
truth, there is no path to follow other than to hate the
evil felt as pervasive, to purify oneself by withdrawal
from contact, and to seek to dominate and subjugate the
powers of evil by the force of one's will. The logic of
Mawdudi's method of argument always follows the rhetorical
pattern of describing the omnipresent evil, of appeal, as
it were, to emotions of horror and despair, and then of a

firm statement of the only conceivable solution--
renunciation of evil ways and total commitment to service
of the good.

Mawdudi thought that this pattern of renunciation
followed by total commitment was essential for all Muslims
because it was, he believed, the pattern exemplified in the
life of the Prophet and the first community of believers.
Sayyid Ahmad Khan, however, rather envisaged the early
Muslims as exemplary because of their reasonableness, their
readiness to forgive, and their emphasis on justice. A
recent study of the Prophet as a diplomat indicates that,
in many of the actual situations of his life, Muhammad had
responded by attempting to resolve disputes by arbitration
and by careful diplomatic procedures.[10] It was this aspect
of the early community's life that was a model for Sayyid
Ahmad Khan.

Mawdudi has claimed that he did not wish to create
sectarianism among Muslims, because he knows that the
community has generally regarded sectarian strife as an
evil to be avoided if the community is to prosper. Yet the
effect of his teaching about other Muslims, his rejection
of other Muslim points of view as wrong and treacherous, is
to initiate a process that tends to disrupt the community.
Under modern conditions, failure to acknowledge the
possibility of diversity of opinion among Muslims tends to
lead to sectarianism. Mawdudi and his followers believe
that uniformity of perspective and ethical stance can be
created among Muslims by persuasion. They expect other
Muslims to repent in response to Mawdudi's teaching, to
make the effort of will to become persons acceptable to
Mawdudi's group of disciples. The common stance is to be
created by conversion and the strengthening of the common
will.

In the medieval period, theologians who held to a
theistic subjectivist position in practice tolerated
Muslims with other interests, particularly sufis. Many of
the medieval theologians were themselves active in the sufi
orders. Yet Mawdudi absolutely opposes sufism as a
betrayal of the correct stance. He does not have the

tolerance, and openness to diversity that characterized
many of the theologians of the Islamic past. As we have
indicated, the theistic subjectivism of the medieval period
was partly a refusal to accept the dogmatism of the
rationalists on certain issues, and an insistence on
leaving certain basic questions unanswered. "Only God
knows" was the pious answer to rationalistic overconfidence
and oversimplification. But the stance of "only God knows"
worked in some measure for tolerance since final decision
and judgment was to be left to God.

The medieval Asharite theologians stressed the
omnipotent God as creator of all that occurs. They
conceived of the divine will as eternally active in
creating and sustaining from moment to moment. They were
baffled about how to permit human freedom when all human
actions stemmed from the creative power of God. They
debated the question, and different schools of thought
arrived at different formulae. The most widely accepted
position was, in a sense, to acknowledge the
unanswerability of the question. The notion of
acquisition, qasb, was used to indicate that humans somehow
acquired responsibility for their actions, even though God
willed the actions.[11] This stalemate, however, remained as
the acknowledgment of a genuine problem that human minds
could not handle. The effort of theology was therefore to
indicate the limitations of the human intelligence. Humans
had to live with an openness towards the end of time when
God would be fully known. In the interim before the end,
the wise were to live good lives, but not to presume to
understand more than they could. Thus, medieval subjective
theism was linked with a firm conviction that ultimate
truth will come only at the end.

Mawdudi does not conceive of God in the manner of the
medieval theologians as one whose will is ultimately
mysterious. He is not preoccupied, as his medieval
predecessors were, with the impossibility of applying human
categories of thought to God. He does not seem concerned
with the intellectual difficulty of knowing the absolute.
Medieval theological writing contains many statements

relating to the inapplicability of human standards of
measurement to Absolute Reality. Mawdudi's writings do not
exhibit a comparable sophistication about the limitations
of human categories of thought. God, for Mawdudi, is not a
mysterious Other whose fullness of being will be
comprehended only at the end of time. He is rather an
engineer with a blueprint for human well-being. Mawdudi's
concerns are related to his fear that immoral persons,
Westerners and rationalist Muslims will corrupt Muslim
society. His stance is that of a protector of threatened
values. Revelation represents to him a safeguard against
these immoral and threatening powers. Clinging to the
authority of revelation is a way of protecting the Muslims
against what is perceived as hostile change. The problem
of morality rather than that of the intellect troubles
Mawdudi. As noted, he feels strongly about the dangers of
sexual licence.

　　With respect to the content of the revelation, the
difference lies in the attitudes to the existing forms of
society. Medieval theologians tended to support the status
quo. They lived in a period in which power rested with
military leaders who governed because of their superior
force. The theologians lived within this system, sometimes
serving as judges or advisors, but often dissociating
themselves to a considerable degree from those actually in
power. The guidance received from revelation was
understood to be a means by which pious persons might
organize their lives so as to meet God on the Judgment Day.
Political leaders were expected to conform as best they
could to the teachings of the religious leaders.
Revelation was understood as supporting existing
structures. Exphasizing human reliance on the creative
power of God tended to mean in practice acceptance of the
attitude that whatever actually happened would have to be
accepted.

　　Mawdudi, on the other hand, assumes that the status
quo of his age is entirely wrong. The content of
revelation is therefore understood by him to mean that
morally upright persons must resist the corrupt status quo

and struggle to implement the true Islamic social order.
Revelation, therefore, implies a will to Islamic
revolution. Any notion of Islamic revolution would have
been foreign to medieval theologians because they did not
understand either the divine or the human will as a force
for revolution. Theistic subjectivism for the medieval
Asharites thus meant acceptance of the world in which the
pious found themselves. Theistic subjectivism in Mawdudi's
case rather means rebellion against the world in which
believers find themselves.

The disputes between the rationalists and
fundamentalists in the modern period are therefore not
simple restatements of the classical disputes between the
Mutazila and the Asharites. The basic reason for the
difference is that modern rationalists and fundamentalists
both assume that the existing forms of society must be
changed. They disagree on "how to" effect these changes,
but they are agreed that change must occur. The
rationalists envisage the process of change as coming about
through the slow processes of reasoning among the believers
as to what appropriate developments ought to be. The
fundamentalists envisage an "Islamic revolution" to be
implemented and directed by the morally sound few. Both
insist that new structures of life must be created.

I will now turn to the question of the relationship of
Mawdudi's position to other modern types of fundamentalism.
James Barr, in his study of Christian fundamentalism, has
maintained that fundamentalism is a phenomenon in the
history of religion that begins with the publication in
1910 of a book about Christianity entitled The
Fundamentals.[12] The persons who have subsequently
manifested attitudes similar to those expressed in that
volume have, in the Christian case, been called
fundamentalists. But the type of ideology is not peculiar
to Christianity. One finds instances of it in all
contemporary religious traditions, as, for example, among
Japanese Buddhists.[13]

Barr maintains that fundamentalism is itself a type of
religion. As such, it is characterized by insistence that

only one interpretation of scripture is acceptable.
Persons accepting the validity of that one interpretation
become emotionally strengthened as they share a form of
group mind. They tend to perceive everyone outside the
group as representative of some form of evil or threatening
power. The contents of the fundamentalist ideology vary.
A group is fundamentalist because of its insistence on the
validity of one interpretation only and because of the
emotional commitment demanded of members of the group.

Mawdudi's position is fundamentalist in these
respects. He does offer only one interpretation of the
Qur'an, as indicated in his commentary. Those who become
members of the group he founded are expected to accept one
interpretation of Islam. Their energy and purposefulness
derive in large measure, I think, from the emotional
strength which comes from membership in a group that has
what Barr calls a self-enclosing ideology.

It is true that certain aspects of Christian
tradition, such as the notion of the Holy Spirit and the
tendency to sectarianism, make Christians even more
vulnerable to fundamentalism than Muslims normally are.
On the other hand, modernity itself is, it would seem, the
main cause of fundamentalism. As Berger has noted, one
side of the coin is the awareness of alienation and threat
posed by the forces of modernity. One response to that
threat is what Berger calls "decisionism," an emphasis on
strengthening the will to uphold, and to fight for what are
perceived as threatened values. The emphasis is on the
will to struggle. "Decisionism" stresses the necessity of
making a decision, a commitment in the face of the menaces
experienced in modernity, and then exercising the will to
implement the values for which one has decided. Anxiety
seems to decrease when one decides to act vigorously in a
certain direction.

There are obviously great strengths in a position of
this kind since it offers clear direction and allows
persons to work purposefully. The difficulties arise,
however, when it may seem that the answers that have been
accepted do not always work out in practice. In Mawdudi's

case, one may note that the direction offered by his group
did not help with the serious difficulties that arose when
the citizens of what was then East Pakistan rose against
the army of West Pakistan, which was attempting to control
them. Those from East Pakistan demanded better treatment
and more recognition of their linguistic, cultural, and
other rights. The upshot of this protest was a civil war
which led to the secession of the East Wing and the
formation of the new nation of Bangladesh. The role of the
Jama'at-i-Islami in the midst of that turmoil and conflict
is an illuminating one. Mawdudi and his followers took the
position that the agitators on the Bengali side had wrong
ideas because they had been influenced by Hindu, communist,
and foreign ideas. Their complaints were seen as a symptom
of evil foreign influence. Mawdudi's remedy for the
troubles in East Pakistan was to urge that the Bengalis be
made into true Muslims.

After the intervention of the West Pakistan Army, the
literature of the Jama'at attacked the Awami League, the
elected party of East Bengal, as part of a world conspiracy
to destroy Islam. The villains were said to be agents of
India, the Christian nations, Jewish expansionism, the
United States, the United Kingdom, and USSR, and so forth.
When the West Pakistan Army entered East Bengal, the
members of the Jama'at-i-Islami co-operated with the
military in efforts to suppress the revolt. The Bengali
resistance movement looked upon the Jama'at workers as the
auxiliaries of the army and fought against them. About one
hundred Jama'at members were killed.[14]

Although the majority of the citizens of the new
nation of Bangladesh were Muslims, they had found against
their fellow Muslims because they had perceived themselves
as discriminated against and exploited. The conflict was
between Muslims. Mawdudi's insistence on labelling the
Bengali Muslims as inferior Muslims dominated by foreign
ideas and customs made him an instrument of one side in the
conflict. His desire to solve the problem by urging the
dissenters to become better Muslims is an illuminating
instance of the inability of the fundamentalists to think

about problems in any other way than in terms of the
paradigm that dominates their minds.

In seeking to understand the basis for an attitude
that tends to consider all those who differ as unclean,
or agents of demonic forces, I have found Iris Murdoch
particularly helpful. She suggests that the basic
realities one is dealing with in studying ethics are not
new or original; the problem is rather to keep on
rediscovering in each new generation insights that have
been found, and lost, and found again. The problems of how
to relate to other persons, how to control anger and greed,
and how to mature in one's grasp of reality have existed as
long as human beings:

> It . . . is an abiding and not a regrettable
> characteristic of the discipline that
> philosophy has in a sense to keep trying to
> return to the beginning. . . . As moral
> agents we have to try to see justly, to
> overcome prejudice, to avoid temptation, to
> control and curb imagination, to direct
> reflection. . . . In particular situations,
> 'reality' as that which is revealed to the
> patient eye of love is an idea entirely
> comprehensible to the ordinary person.[15]

The person moving away from morality is thus one who
does not try to see justly, nor to overcome prejudice, nor
to control imagination, nor to direct reflection. Such
persons, in her terminology, tend to be dominated by their
personal fantasies; they often fail to respond
constructively to the real situations around them. A
person dominated by fantasy, for example, may see another
person as little more than the manifestation of the devil
that preoccupies his or her mind. Those who think like
this usually recognize few moral obligations to the other
person. If the other has reality only as a phase of one's
own fantasy, he or she can easily be despised or cast out.

A further complication is that one person's fantasies
may be projected into the minds of other individuals or
groups, who may then become dominated by the fantasies of
the first person. They all then react to the other persons
they meet as little more than aspects of the original
fantasy. The group mind of the fundamentalists is usually
influenced by certain strong fantasies, particularly about

evil forces that threaten them. Rather than striving to
overcome their prejudices and to take other persons with
differing views seriously, fundamentalists
characterisitically fantasize about the others as
instruments of some evil plot or power.

   We all have self-protective and self-promoting
fantasies. Iris Murdoch's point is that serious morality
requires us to be trying all the time to let reality
impinge on us, and to overcome our fantasies. To argue in
this way is not to deny that Muslims in fact often have real
enemies in the modern world, not least because of the
centuries of Western antagonism towards Islam. But Sayyid
Ahmad Khan was certainly aware of the hostility. His
method was to try to use reason to persuade those who were
hostile to change their minds and to encourage his fellow
Muslims to achieve such eminent positions as skilled
persons that they would inevitably elicit respect. To
respond to antagonism with reason requires a high degree of
self-confidence.

   Iris Murdoch refers in another book to the
iconoclastic tendencies of Islamic art as another instance
of a cultural effort to repress fantasy and to encourage an
openness to the world. Islamic art, she contends,
discerns, emphasizes, and extends the harmonious rhythm of
divine creation. It produces good design rather than
pretentious rival objects.[16] The Qur'anic virtues, such as
patience and sobriety, are very similar to the Platonic
ones. Both sources teach that a good person has to keep on
trying very hard to be just when he or she is judging an
actual situation; one must not be dominated by his or her
emotions. The Qur'an warns believers not to favour
relatives when one attempts to arrive at just decisions.
Insights of this kind are probably shared by almost all
cultures, but they are particularly emphasized in
traditions like Platonism and Islam which seek to provide a
basis for a universal human order.

   The contrast between Sayyid Ahmad Khan's condemnation
of bigotry as a major source of evil in individual and
social life and Mawdudi's rejection of kufr, understood as

any individual or society with ideas different from those
of himself and his group, is of major significance. Both
terms are part of the Islamic heritage. The difference
lies in how the terms are to be applied. Who is to be
labelled an unbeliever, a rejector of God's truth, or a
bad person? What crimes deserve this condemnation?

Mawdudi uses kufr as he does because his imagination
has been seized by a vision of himself and his followers
re-enacting the original conquests and successes of the
Prophet and the first Caliphs. Kufr in this respect means
to reject this image of what Islam is and what must be
done.

In Sayyid Ahmad Khan's view a bigot is one who fails
to do justice to other persons. The English who were
racists and contemptuous of Indian culture and tradition
were bigots, as were those Muslims who despised foreign
culture without making any effort to understand it.
Bigotry also existed among those Muslims who were loud in
condemning any view other than their own.

Peter Hardy has told us how repulsive and
unsympathetic the British appeared to many
nineteenth-century Muslims.

> Eaters of pork and drinkers of wine, who paraded
> their women in the bare-shouldered evening
> fashions of the early Victorian age, builders of
> graceless bungalows, unskilled in the Ghazal,
> always counting their--or worse, other
> people's--money, and contemptuous of what they
> did not understand, the British added
> boorishness and arrogance, scandalous laxity and
> repulsive habits to their undoubted
> infidelity.[17]

The extent of Sayyid Ahmad Khan's courage and
resourcefulness becomes the more apparent when we consider
the appearances of the foreign world he wished to encounter
with peaceful and reasoned discourse. Great diplomats need
courage as well as confidence in the reasonableness of all
human beings, no matter how strange their appearance.

In comparing the thought of Sayyid Ahmad Khan and
Mawdudi, I have tried to indicate that both these ethical
stances draw from the storehouse of the Islamic past,
although both are also new. The wisdom of temperance is

one facet of the Islamic ethical tradition, well
represented, for example, in the writings of Ibn Miskiwaih.
The call to revolution is also part of the tradition,
illustrated by the original revolution implemented by the
Prophet and his followers, and stressed again in recent
times by the various reformist groups such as the Wahabis.
Both models have existed and have been effective at
different phases of Islamic history.

The discontinuity with the medieval past lies
particularly in the effort made possible through increased
literacy to involve the general populace of Muslims in
these debates of the meaning and purpose of Islam. Both
Sayyid Ahmad Khan and Mawdudi envisage a future in which
Muslims will be self-conscious to an unprecedented degree:
they will have a new awareness of what they are striving to
express through their common life. The issue of the
meaning of consensus arises here. Within the traditional
formal procedures adopted by the jurists, consensus was a
principle of jurisprudence in the sense of consensus of the
jurists. The notion of reopening discussion about the
values to be implemented through Islamic social structures
carries with it in the thought of both these modern
thinkers the new idea of involving all the people in the
discussion.

Sayyid Ahmad Khan's vision of an improved social order
is essentially optimistic. He considers the movement away
from the Muslim and other forms of medieval despotism to be
progressive because people will have a greater opportunity
to live under structures of law that will protect them from
the ravages of despots. He is interested in written
constitutions and written law as modes of protection. He
also sees the democratic participation of all citizens as
another way of protecting individuals from abuse. From his
perspective, the movement of Muslim civilizations away from
medieval forms of despotism is related to the similar
movements of other civilizations. He sees the progress of
Muslim civilization as part of a wider change within human
history as a whole away from arbitrary tyranny.

Mawdudi does not share this optimism. I noted in my

earlier quotation from al-Ghazali the reference to the
Qur'anic verse that indicates that God may ultimately
intend that conflicting parties may be reconciled.
Al-Ghazali indicates that his verse means that Muslims must
struggle very hard to be just to their opponents and to
strive for reconciliation. Mawdudi, however, in his survey
of Islamic history, dismisses the sufis as other-worldly
dreamers who falsified true Islam. He has little positive
to say about sufi influence. Hence al-Ghazali would not be
an examplar for him as he was for Sayyid Ahmad Khan.
Mawdudi does not place a high value on reconciliation, or
conflict resolution. He rather emphasises the need to
resist and to overthrow evil systems, and to implement the
one good system. His pessimism reflects despair.

Mawdudi's notion of virtue does not include the idea
of exercising control over response to abuse. His writings
are rather full of condemnation and even caricatures of
those he does not agree with. He responds to Western
condemnation of Islam by condemning Western civilization
even more strongly. Since some Western writers condemn
Muslims for veiling their women, Mawdudi responds by urging
that Western civilization is so perverse that marriages
take place with both parties nude. This instance of his
way of responding to attack illustrates the fundamental
characteristics of his way of thinking. Virtue to him also
means an active force of personality, but in his case the
action is to take the form of withdrawal from involvement
from all evil persons and structures so that a new and pure
way of life can be created.

Mawdudi perceives the persons and structures around
him as so perverse that they must be overthrown by a
transformed way of life. His appeal is for total change of
hearts. Those who respond to his call are to abandon their
old ways of life and to become transformed, and hence
moral, persons. Virtue in this perspective can only follow
from a change of heart and from a commitment to
implementation of the new ideal. The new ideal is directed
ultimately toward the well-being of everyone else since it
is intended to make clear before the eyes of unenlightened

and wicked people what a good life truly is. Mawdudi's
understanding of morality is thus that the good people must
organize themselves and act positively to implement the
virtues they believe in. His invitation is essentially a
call to direct one's will toward the active implementation
of the social order he envisages.

Society has different connotations for these two
Muslim thinkers. For the rationalist, it is conceived of
as heterogeneous; for the fundamentalist, as homogeneous.
Thus, Sayyid Ahmad Khan envisaged the processes of change
as working slowly through diverse layers of the complex
social reality. Legislative organs of the state, judicial
bodies, educational bodies, commercial organizations, and
voluntary associations of citizens were all involved with
differing and varied problems. Any one aspect of social
life, such as changing the way history was taught, or a
court decision, or a new mode of production, might have
repercussions on other aspects of the community's common
life. Sayyid Ahmad Khan's greater optimism was perhaps
linked to his feeling that there would always by something
constructive to be done in some areas of life even if
others were blocked off or repressive. Thus, foreign
domination might have unpleasant aspects, but Muslims could
still carry on and be effective in other parts of their
society. Governmental administration was only one among
many other segments of the heterogeneous society.

Mawdudi, however, thought of society as one rigorously
integrated organic whole. His belief in authority stemmed
from his conviction that the head of the society, the Amir,
should directly shape and control every aspect of the
common life of the people. Thus, society conceived of as
an homogeneous body was necessarily either totally bad or
totally good. All the organs of the state would have to
react to the same chords played by the same player.
Mawdudi did not conceive of a healthy society as one in
which a variety of different processes might be going on
with relatively little to do with each other. Such variety
would have meant chaos from the perspective of his manner
of envisaging the social organism.

Sayyid Ahmad Khan, in company with liberals from other traditions, welcomed change; he did not preach a return to the loose organization of the medieval world. He particularly welcomed Montesquieu's teachings about the superiority of written law as a way to improve human rights and human well-being.[18] In my opinion, he called for a modern society that would have a degree of heterogeneity. This society would differ in many significant respects from the medieval order. There would be more centralization of law and administration. But the state would not be the only effective form of organization. Sayyid Ahmad Khan's lifelong involvement with voluntary associations of one kind and another indicates that he envisaged the modern society as a multisegmented reality. He did not suppose that moral well-being necessarily emanated only from the top.

In fact, Sayyid Ahmad Khan's comment that constitutional government is better than despotism may be taken to indicate that he believed that the removal of the medieval form of domination by one ruler was an advance. To believe in the value of constitutional government means to distrust the notion of any single authority imposing his will from the top down and to prefer written guarantees that those lower on the social scale will have mechanisms by which they can make their voices effectively heard. Such a system rests on the assumption that the moral guidance may well come from outside those actually in power. If citizens can form voluntary associations to work for the implementation of their convictions, they are not dependent on any superior power to get their ideas realized. The example of Sayyid Ahmad Khan bringing forth a new institution of education for Muslims through the work of volunteers is an effective instance of reform from below. The conservative Muslims who implemented their own new form of training religious leaders at Deoband were also working through volunteers and not through state-controlled mechanisms.[19]

Sayyid Ahmad Khan seems to have understood that participating in voluntary associations concerned to

resolve some problems was a useful way, not only of
influencing the shaping of policy, but also of training
character. One who sits on a committee working with others
to think through and to work for a common purpose gradually
gets his animality transformed into humanity. One has to
listen to the points of view of others and respond
reasonably. One learns to hear the criticisms of one's
own position and becomes aware of the need to discover
consensus as a reality different from the arbitrary opinion
of one. That consensus was one of the principles of
classical Muslim jurisprudence indicates that the members
of the community were familiar with the notion that what
was truly acceptable ought to be intelligible to more than
one mind.

Sayyid Ahmad Khan urged the Muslims of his generation
to overcome their unthinking prejudices and to learn to
think objectively about the needs of the world. He was
convinced that training in dispassionate reasoning was the
only effective way to shape future generations so that they
would be able to solve real problems. Unless persons learn
to reason together realistically, they will not be able
effectively to change the world for the better. Unless
they could overcome prejudice, they would not be vital.

> A man cannot satisfy all his wants himself.
> As a social being, he requires the help and
> support of others. But due to his bigotry,
> he turns dissatisfied against his own people
> and is not inclined to form friendship with
> anyone except those who think and feel like
> him. . . .

> Man who is free from bigotry seeks perfection
> in every aspect of life, but a bigot cannot
> attain any excellence . . . because he has
> pre-conceived prejudicial notions which he is
> not prepared to modify. In short, he is blind
> to values, knowledge, truth and humanity. . . .
> Bigotry has brought about the fall of nations
> and has sapped their vitality in the course of
> centuries. . . . As firm believers in religion
> we should eliminate bigotry from our hearts,
> because all human beings are our brothers. We
> should love all, be truthful to all, have
> friendship with all, and wish the good of all.
> . . . The main characteristic of a bigot is
> that he is puffed up with pride and does not
> condescend to maintain friendly contact with

fellow-beings. Arrogance creates blindness in
his perception of things and pride leads him
to his doom.[20]

The statement "is not inclined to form friendships
with anyone except those who think and feel like him"
indicates that voluntary associations such as those Sayyid
Ahmad Khan worked with were not expected to be sects or
affinity groups. An affinity group in which all have the
same ideas is not a problem-solving association. In the
latter, differences of opinion are real and are worked out.
Persons work to pursue a common purpose, such as the
promotion of science, or of educational reform, or the
promotion of the Urdu language. The group is not an end in
itself. When the problem has been solved, the association
has no further reason to exist. Persons come to the
association because of their interest in a particular
problem, but they may also be simultaneously members of
many other groups and have other interests. A
problem-solving voluntary association is not the centre and
dominating reality in an individual's life, whereas a sect
or affinity group may control his whole existence. The
sect functions to protect the individual from persons with
ideas and feelings different from his; it may try to
control his thinking on every aspect of life. A sect or
affinity group is an association of those who are generally
unwilling to form friendships with those who differ from
them. Sayyid Ahmad Khan considered that attitude bigotry.

I began this book with the statement that moralities
are languages of persuasion, using various forms of
rhetoric to invoke agreement. I have argued that both
Sayyid Ahmad Khan and Mawdudi have been extremely
persuasive advocates of their respective positions among
their fellow Muslims. Both of them have been striving to
create a new consensus among Muslims. The effort to create
consensus is itself legitimated by the Islamic past, since
the Prophet himself laboured to work co-operatively with
his co-religionists, and since the notion of consensus is a
fundamental principle of Islamic jurisprudence.[21] Muslims
agree that consensus ought to exist. They do not
necessarily agree on how consensus is to be arrived at.

As I see it, the differences between the two ethical
stances under consideration lie both in the understanding
of human virtues and in the respective visions of ideal
social structures. I share with the poet Hali considerable
respect for the moral wisdom of Sayyid Ahmad Khan's mother.
The sources are agreed that she exerted a remarkable
influence on him, especially with respect to training him
not to respond to abuse with vituperation. His lifework
was a struggle to overcome the contempt which the British
had for the Muslims and the hostility which the Muslims had
for the British. Virtue in this context meant to work to
transcend antagonisms and to strive for mutual respect.
Such virtue is an active force of personality that requires
self-knowledge and self-discipline. Since the source of
this understanding of virtue was Sayyid Ahmad Khan's
mother, it is manifestly a thoroughly Islamic perspective
with respect to human maturation. I think that it is
particularly a stance representative of the values of the
administrative governing classes to which his mother
belonged.

Mawdudi, in my view, does not have a similarly
optimistic view of the possibility of reconciliation among
conflicting perspectives. He is rather profoundly
pessimistic about the possibilities for improvement of
human life within the existing, or emerging social and
political orders. His version of world history teaches
that nothing but the implementation of the social order he
envisages will lead to a good life for human beings. Any
other way of life that has existed, or might exist, is, he
thinks, inherently demonic and destructive of the good
life. His urgent call for reform carries with it the
insistence that all other ways of life are entirely bad.
Mawdudi wants to protect citizens from abuse by ensuring
that those who exercise governing powers will be morally
trustworthy. He thus envisages good government to be a
kind of paternalistic control of the many by the
trustworthy few. As we noted, he advocates extreme
punishment for crimes such as adultery so that the rest of
the populace can be guided by their leaders away from the

dangerous temptations that might disrupt the family and the
social order.

I have tried thus far to describe these two positions
without drawing conclusions as to which is more
representative of the Islamic tradition, or more right.
Since Mawdudi is the more recent ethical thinker, he is the
more popular now in the sense that his ideas are very much
alive particularly among Muslim university students. Much
of what Sayyid Ahmad Khan advocated, such as attendance at
universities, has been taken up by the Muslims generally;
hence it is no longer provocative. The process by which
Muslim consensus operates is often not measurable directly.
For example, when Sayyid Ahmad Khan first advocated
changing customs, his views were considered radical and
threatening to traditional Muslim life by many.
Nevertheless, Muslim societies have gradually accepted many
of the innovations he put forward, particularly with
respect to education, and with respect to the acceptance of
constitutions and written codes of law. One can tell that
consensus has operated after the fact, but not before. In
every Muslim nation, jurists and legislatures have been at
work gradually transforming the legal codes. The process
has been gradual, and it has sometimes taken the form of
selecting from the variety of past positions values that
seem more acceptable now. This is not to say that the
jurists have taken the same positions in all Muslim
countries, but it is to say that they have all been using
various forms of reasoning in adapting their legal
structures to perceived new demands and needs. In this
matter, consensus has followed the direction indicated by
Sayyid Ahmad Khan.

Whether it is more appropriate for a Muslim to be an
optimist or a pessimist is a question which brings to mind
William James' thesis in The Varieties of Religious
Experience.[22] He maintained that optimism and pessimism
are two types of religiousness that one finds everywhere
and that are not explicable other than by noting that
personalities have tendencies of the one kind or the other.
I have been arguing that the optimism of Sayyid Ahmad Khan

is related to his rationality in that he trusts that other
people will be able to grasp and to accept a reasonable
point of view. Mawdudi also maintains that his is open to
reason and that he is willing to listen to the arguments of
anyone who can attempt to convince him. He says that he
would change his views if he could be convinced. The two
positions might look similar in this respect; they are
similar in that neither rejects human reasoning out of
hand. The difference lies in a certain flexibility of
mind. Mawdudi's pessimism is rooted in his distrust of
anyone who will not become entirely converted to his
perspective. Mawdudi assumes there must be one right
position. Sayyid Ahmad Khan did not think that one perfect
system must, or could exist.

Sayyid Ahmad Khan experienced from his fellow
believers acceptance of some of his projects, translation
of books on science, for example, and the creation of a
university, whereas others of his ideas, especially with
respect to interpretation of scripture, were not widely
accepted or understood. He did not put all his notions
into one package that had to be accepted or rejected as a
whole. Neither did he form a group of supporters who were
expected to agree with him in every respect. He worked
with many different kinds of persons for many different
causes. He left no disciples in the sense of individuals
who agreed with all his ideas. He thus understood
rationality to operate in a pluralistic society,
pluralistic even among Muslims, in which many different
opinions and affirmations would co-exist. Reason was to be
used to persuade people to change their ways, but not to
shape them into a common mould. One facet of modernity is
that individuals have much greater freedom to choose their
own ways of life and thought. Sayyid Ahmad Khan was
concerned to guide individuals to use their freedom
constructively, but he was not acting as an authority
figure whose values must be imposed. The history of the
inner life of the Aligarh College which he founded shows
that it was in many respects a tumultous mixture of values
and perspectives.[23] Sayyid Ahmad Khan was a force there,

but he was one among many strong voices, and he by no means
always dominated.

Mawdudi, on the other hand, puts forth an ideology
that is intended to be accepted or rejected as a whole
package. He said he would change his mind if he could be
convinced of the validity of a point. But to change
details does not alter the fact that there must be one
package, and the package as a whole must be accepted or
rejected. Mawdudi intends his followers to be models for
the whole Muslim community and, ultimately, for the world.
They are to be trained to be so morally upright that their
virtues will guide humanity out of the darkness and
perversity into which it has fallen. Consensus is to
operate from this perspective in a paternalistic manner:
once the morally sound people have power, it is assumed
that their virtues will be so self-evident that the others
will be converted to their ways.

Which of these two perspectives will prove to be more
enduring is a question that remains open at present. Both
types of ethical stance are present among Muslims--as they
are among persons in other societies. The most probable
result is that a form of pluralism will go on in which a
diversity of ethical stances will continue to exist among
Muslims. The words of Ibn Miskiwaih appear most
appropriate:

> Virtue can be achieved only by association. We
> have made it clear . . . that man, of all the
> animals, cannot attain his perfection by
> himself alone. He must have recourse to the
> help of a great number of people in order to
> achieve a good life and follow the right path.
> This is why the philosophers have said: Man is
> a civic being by nature. This means that he
> needs to live in a city with a large population
> in order to achieve human happiness. Every man
> needs other people by nature as well as by
> necessity. He must, therefore, be friendly
> towards others, associate well with them, and
> hold them in sincere affection, for they
> complement him and complete his humanity; and
> he himself plays the same role in their lives.
> . . . For he who does not mingle with other
> people and who does not live with them in
> cities cannot show temperance, intrepidity,
> liberality, or justice. . . .

. . . But virtues are not non-existences;
they are actions and deeds which are
manifested when one participates and lives
with other people, and has dealings and
various kinds of associations with them.
Indeed, we teach and learn the human
virtues by the aid of which we live and
mingle with other people, so that we may
attain, from and by these virtues, other
kinds of happiness when we pass to
another state which does not exist for us
at present.
       Here ends the first discourse, with the
praise of God and by His grace.[24]

Despite the discontinuity in many respects between
medieval and modern ways of life and thought, these
affirmations of Ibn Miskiwaih are still relevant. The
attitude exemplified here is like that of Sayyid Ahmad Khan
because of the emphasis on the need for mutuality among
citizens. The weakness of the fundamentalist position
seems to me to lie in an exaggerated claim to wisdom. The
assumption that a few are wise and good enough to exercise
unquestioned and unrestricted authority over the rest of
the community is open to serious question. Sayyid Ahmad
Khan would not have accepted that position: his belief
that we truly need other people to complement ourselves
suggests that we can and should have sincere relationships
with others who do not necessarily agree with us in all
respects. Mawdudi, on the other hand, can relate to other
people only as his followers or as his enemies. His
position requires either that one convert to his views, or
that one is a bad person. Ibn Miskiwaih may not have
envisaged a twentieth-century form of culturally pluralist
society, yet his teaching of the need to co-exist justly
with others in order to learn temperance from them
certainly indicates that he thought of individuals as
constantly maturing as they learned to take seriously
persons who were different from themselves. If one
considers temperance a virtue, it follows that one
envisages a society in which differences are real.

Many of Mawdudi's followers would say that to tolerate
evil behaviour is a form of weakness. One can certainly
argue that a passionate concern for the betterment of
society should lead one to fight actively against all forms

of wickedness that one discerns. I am not suggesting that
the differences of opinion between those who advocate
tolerance and diversity and those who are driven by
reforming zeal are going to disappear. I would rather say
that diverse ethical stances on such issues as alcoholism
and the breakdown of family life have existed before among
Muslims--and in other cultures too. But alcoholism and the
breakdown of family life are just two of the facets of
contemporary industrialised society that many Muslims find
threatening. The appeal of Mawdudi's position lies in
insistence that all evils of this kind can be kept out if
Muslims will submit themselves to his guidance. The
greater pessimism he reflects may indicate a greater fear
that Muslim values will collapse unless the foreign is
removed. Sayyid Ahmad Khan optimistically thought that
Muslims would be able to see for themselves which values to
change, and which to keep. In this respect, the issue is
whether the majority are to be trusted to think for
themselves, or whether they have to be submitted to
effective political control by their moral leaders. This
dilemma, of course, is as present in the liberal
democracies as it is in the Muslim world; the problem of
deciding between the two positions is not peculiar to
Muslims.

    A central problem is how to combat the forces that are
perceived as evil. A recent Christian theologian writing
about the ethics of Christology has expressed a point of
view that seems to me closer to the Muslim emphasis on
conscience than some earlier forms of Christian ethical
thought. He offers to define ethics as "that realm of life
which has to do with matters of conscience. It therefore
includes the social formation of conscience, its occasional
transformations in the individual and society, and the
problems inherent in acting conscientiously."[25]

    From this perspective, which seems entirely in harmony
with the Muslim notion of akhlaq understood as the effort
to provide means to keep human virtues in their optimum
state, it follows that to combat evil includes taking
responsibility for the social formation of conscience.

This involves all forms of moral education, and it also
bears on all the structures of society. Those who are
oppressed cannot be expected to be just or generous. If
they manage to achieve those perspectives, their moral
victory is to their credit, but the responsibility of the
oppressors to remove the structures of injustice remains
urgent. As Ghazali said, we are responsible for the
well-being of our sisters and brothers. Since he was an
eleventh-century man, he did not have the awareness we have
of the possibilities of transforming conditions of life in
the world. But his conscience, I think, was as lucid as
anyone's has ever been. Evil has to be combatted in the
self and in society. In the self, its worst forms are
self-centredness, anger, lust, and greed. In society, evil
is in the structures of injustice and inhumanity.

We have suggested that many modern Muslims see
Mawdudi's perspective as the one most conducive to a form
of jihad (effort) against the forces of disintegration and
evil that they fear. It should be remembered, however,
that Sayyid Ahmad Khan was also a fighter. As we indicated
in his remarks on the necessity of imposing small pox
vaccination on people, he did not hesitate to take strong
measures when he thought them necessary. He was willing to
do his fighting through voluntary associations as well as
through the powers of the legislative bodies. He did not
believe that the good and sensible people needed
necessarily to have political power in order to fight
effectively to get important changes made. There is a
great deal of precedent for this position in the Islamic
past. The devout persons who first collected hadith and
who worked out the principles of jurisprudence did so as
participants in something like voluntary associations
rather than as tools in the hands of the wielders of power
in the state.

The emphasis in the fundamentalist position on control
of the state as the only effective means to constructive *aim*
change is exaggerated. Iqbal said that the ultimate sin of
Islam was the implementation of a spiritual democracy.[26]
The accomplishment of that goal requires a genuine

participation of all citizens rather than the imposition of
the views of any one person or group on the others.

Berger has commented that the emphasis on will is
characteristic of the neo-orthodox position in the
Christian case as in other modern forms of neo-orthodoxy.[27]
That perspective proved particularly effective as a
rallying point for Christians who were reacting against the
Nazi domination of Germany. Nevertheless it did not
continue to be equally persuasive. The call to persons to
surrender their reason is perhaps effective under modern
conditions mainly in periods or situations of extreme
stress. We also find appeals to commit the will to the
service of what is perceived as the immanent force of
history among revolutionaries of many kinds. Mawdudi, in
this respect, is assuming that the experience of
revolutionaries is a paradigm for Muslims. Sayyid Ahmad
Khan, on the other hand, began his original thinking on the
basis of a conviction that the emotional zeal of the
revolutionaries who had died fighting in 1831 had been
misguided. In the modern context, the issue is between
commitment of the will to a direction given by an
authoritative leader, or group, and an acceptance of an
open society in which diversity of thought and practice
will be acknowledged as legitimate.

The popularity of Mawdudi's views at present may be
seen as part of a current increase in the popularity of
fundamentalist positions in all the religious traditions.
The appeal to decisionism and to submission to the
authority of those conceived of as morally upright leaders
is extremely attractive to many persons in the context of
the severe dilemmas of the late twentieth century.
Mawdudi's idea that God is an engineer with a plan is a
twentieth century way of thinking. In his emphasis on the
need to follow an enlightened group who are the bearers of
a plan, Mawdudi reasons as do many other twentieth century
revolutionary leaders. The idea that the plan is immanent
in the historical process, and that the leaders are needed
to make the inevitable come true is a mode of reasoning
characteristic of those who argue that control of society

must be put in their hands.

Sayyid Ahmad Khan did not ask Muslims to put him or
his friends in power. He did ask them to learn new skills,
and to open themselves to astonishing new forms of
knowledge, such as those provided by modern astronomy. He
wanted them to expand the horizons of their minds. He also
hoped that the evils of medieval forms of despotism were to
be transcended. Thus he urged Muslims to implement forms
of government in which individuals would be protected from
arbitrary tyranny. His knowledge of what life had been
like under the despots of medieval India made him very
concerned to urge his fellow believers to work towards
forms of social organization in which individuals could be
protected from the dominance and interference of the state
in their lives. Even when he thought the state should
interfere, as in legislating compulsory vaccination, he
wanted this done in a way that would cause as little
distress as possible to the citizens. This could be done
by educating the citizens to see for themselves the value
of the laws, and also by imposing the laws in a way that
caused as little offense as possible.

Mawdudi has said that the enforcement of severe
punishments such as flogging for sexual crimes should
"terrify the whole population so that no one can dare
commit it."[28] Sayyid Ahmad Khan wanted to persuade Muslims
to see the value of a law such as compulsory vaccination;
even in such a case, he disliked to impose law unless the
citizens were fully aware of its need. He profoundly
distrusted despots; in practice, this meant that he knew, as
a practising magistrate as well as an historian, that power
can easily be misused, and that the powerless always need
protection. Mawdudi's intent to terrify the population
into seeing the moral worth of his position is more
reminiscent of the despots than it is of the reasonableness
of Sayyid Ahmad Khan. One may well comment that when
people are terrified into obeying a law, they obey not of
their free will, nor of their moral insight, but simply out
of their terror.

I find this notion of terrifying people into obedience

incompatible with the general thrust of Muslim ethical
thought. It suggests lack of concern for those who are
punished, and for those who are to be terrorised into
being good. The dignity of the persons to be so treated
is not being respected. I understand Muslim ethical
thought to have stressed eqalitarianism, and the
encouragement of a sensitive conscience within the
individual. Terror does not breed a sensitive conscience.
No child becomes an autonomous and morally responsible
adult if he or she has been too much intimidated. The
nourishing of morally responsible adults requires the
cultivation of persons for whom autonomy is an experienced
reality.

Al-Ghazali is rightly among the most revered of Muslim
religious thinkers because of the impact of his thought on
generations of Muslims. The respect in which he had been
held certainly reflects the view that he internalised the
vision he had received from the Qur'an, and the example of
the Prophet so effectively that generations of devout
Muslims have recognised authority in his teaching on how to
live in response to God's gracious revelation of his nature
and his purpose for humanity. In his volume On
Brotherhood, al-Ghazali speaks in great detail of the need
for respect for the dignity of the fellow believers, and of
the very great necessity of practising continual
self-examination with respect to one's attitude to the
others; an unceasing process should go on of purging
oneself of all temptation to vilify, to abuse, and to
condemn the others. This process is necessary because the
pride of the individual who wants to justify himself or
herself by condemning the others has to be uprooted from
the soul. In al-Ghazali's diagnosis of the human
condition, pride obscures the soul, and God. The believer
must root pride out of his, or her soul, if he, or she is
to become capable of free response to God, and to the
fellow believers. The on-going devotional life of Muslim
believers continues to nourish this sense of the need to
transcend autonomous pride, and to recover trust in the
goodness of God.

One can understand that for those impatient to change society, and to implement as fast as possible what they imagine will be a more just and humane economic and social order, such concerns as those of al-Ghazali might seem obscurantist, or irrelevant to the serious issues of social change. The life of Sayyid Ahmad Khan himself is, however, an indication that a person who internalised the same virtues as those commended by al-Ghazali could yet be an activist in social causes. It can even be argued that Sayyid Ahmad Khan was more effective as a social reformer because he did not vilify his opponents.

The cumulative tradition of Muslim ethical thought has stressed, and continues to stress eqalitarianism, equity and equilibrium as individual and social virtues. These virtues have been understood as reflections within human beings of the attributes of their creator. Since God is understood to be characterised by unfailing mercy, justice and goodness, human beings as they come to comprehend these attributes through their devotional lives must express them through the structures of their individual and corporate existences. Thus an individual Muslim is to be merciful, just and good, and a Muslim social order is to make possible the implementation and encouragement of these virtues. How this is to be done has been and remains the challenge which Muslims have accepted, and with which they continue to struggle, to live, and to pray.

Notes

Notes to Chapter 1:

[1]Frederick Bird, "Paradigms and Parameters for the Comparative Study of Religious and Ideological Ethics," Journal of Religious Ethics 19/2 (Fall 1981) pp. 159, 160.

[2]For a discussion of cumulative tradition see W.C. Smith, The Meaning and End of Religion (New York: MacMillan, 1963).

[3]Yvonne Yazbeck Haddad, Contemporary Islam and the Challenge of History (Albany: State University of New York Press, 1982), pp. 4-12. See also Fazlur Rahman "Roots of Islamic Neo-Fundamentalism" in Philip H. Stoddard, Cuttrell and Margaret W. Sullivan, eds., Change and the Muslim World (Syracuse University Press, 1981), pp. 23-39.

[4]See three review articles of the book Comparative Religious Ethics: A New Method by David Little and Sumner B. Twiss in Religious Studies Review 6/4, pp. 289-306. The reviewers are Jeffrey Stout, Edmund A. Santurri and Donald K. Swearer.

[5]James Sellers, Theological Ethics (New York, MacMillan, 1966), pp. 3-4.

[6]Hans Wehr, A dictionary of Modern Written Arabic (Ithaca, N.Y.: Cornell University Press, 1961), pp. 258-59.

[7]George F. Hourani, Islamic Rationalism, The Ethics of Abd al-Jabbar (Oxford, Clarendon Press, 1971), pp. 3, 4. See also Dwight M. Donaldson, Studies in Muslim Ethics (London, S.P.C.K., 1953).

[8]Marshall Hodgson, The Venture of Islam, 3 vols. (Chicago, University of Chicago Press, 1974).

[9]J. Baljon, Modern Muslim Koran Interpretation (Leiden: Brill, 1964).

[10]For a discussion of the significance of eschatological orientations, see Peter Slater, The Dynamics of Religion (New York: Harper & Row, 1978), pp. 64-78.

[11]Fazlur Rahman, Major Themes of the Qur'an (Chicago, Bibliotheca Islamica, 1980).

[12]All the quotations from the Qur'an are from A.J. Arberry, The Koran Interpreted (London, Oxford University Press, reprinted 1975). Surah I.

[13]Marcel Boisard, L'Humanisme de l'Islam (Paris, Albin Michel, 1979), pp. 58-72.

[14]Ibid., pp. 98, 99.

[15]Keith Critchlow, Islamic Patterns (London, Thames & Hudson, 1976).

[16]N.J. Coulson, A history of Islamic Law (Edinburgh, Edinburgh University Press, 1972).

[17]Fazlur Rahman, Islamic Methodology in History (Karachi, Central Institute of Islamic Research, 1965), p. 149.

[18]Ibid., pp. 11-15.

[19]Ibid., pp. 19, 20.

[20]George F. Hourani, "Ethics in Medieval Islam: A Conspectus," in George F. Hourani, ed., Essays on Islamic Philosophy and Science (Albany, State University of New York Press, 1975), p. 129.

[21]F. Rahman, Islamic Methodology in History, pp. 23-24.

[22]George F. Hourani, Islamic Rationalism, The Ethics of 'Abd al-Jabbar, (Oxford, Clarendon Press, 1971), p. 3.

[23]Ibid., pp. 132-137.

[24]Hourani, "Ethics in Medieval Islam," p. 134.

[25]George F. Hourani, The Ethics of Abd al-Jabbar, pp. 12, 13.

[26]Ibid., pp. 11, 12.

[27]Ibid., p. 30.

[28]C.K. Zurayk, trans., The Refinement of Character: A translation from the Arabic of Ahmad ibn Muhammad Miskaway Tadhib al-Akhlaq (Beirut, The American University of Beirut, 1968), pp. 52, 53.

[29]Ibid., p. 127.

[30]Marshall Hodgson, The Venture of Islam, vol. 2, pp. 201-254.

[31]Anne Marie Schimmel, The Mystical Dimension of Islam (Chapel Hill, University of North Carolina Press, 1975), pp. 228-236.

[32]Muhtar Holland, trans., Al-Ghazali on the Duties of
Brotherhood (Woodstock, N.Y., The Overlook Press, 1976),
pp. 36, 37, 41, 47, 69; See also Bankey Behari, trans., The
Revival of the Religious Sciences by al-Ghazali (London,
The Camelot Press, 1964); F.R.C. Bagley, trans., Ghazali's
Book of Council for Kings (London, Oxford University Press,
1964).

Notes to Chapter 2:

[1]K.A. Nizami, Sayyid Ahmad Khan (Publications
Division, Ministry of Information and Broadcasting,
Government of India, 1966), p. 101.

[2]Major-General G.F.I. Graham, The Life and Work of Sir
Syed Ahmed Khan (Karachi, Oxford University Press,
reprinted 1974), pp. 97-102.

[3]B.A. Dar, Religious Thought of Sayyid Ahmad Khan
(Lahore, Institute of Islamic Culture, 1957), p. 2.

[4]Shan Mohammed, ed., Writings and Speeches of Sir Syed
Ahmed Khan (Bombay, Nacheket Publications, 1972), p. 12.

[5]Hafeez Malik and Morris Dembo, trans., Sir Sayyid
Ahmad Khan's History of the Bijnore Rebellion (Published by
the Asian Studies Center, Michigan State University, n.d.),
pp. 48, 49.

[6]Shan Mohammed, ed., Writings, pp. 15-33.

[7]Graham, The Life and Work of Sir Syed Ahmed Khan, p.
103.

[8]Ibid., pp. 89, 82.

[9]Ibid., p. 103.

[10]Fazlur Rahman, Islamic Methodology in History, p.
169.

[11]Muhammad Abdullah Khan Khushgi, ed., Maqalat-i-Sir
Syed (Aligarh, National Printers, 1952), pp. 40-49, 93-113.

[12]Graham, The Life and Work of Sir Syed Ahmed Khan, pp.
157-158.

[13]Muhammad Abdullah Khan Khushgi, ed., Maqalat-i-Sir
Syed, pp. 60-66, 93-113.

[14]Christian W. Troll, Sayyid Ahmad Khan, A
Reinterpretation of Muslim Theology (New Delhi, Vikas
Publishing House, 1978), pp. 254. 255.

[15]Graham, The Life and Work of Sir Syed Ahmed Khan, p.
84.

[16] Qeyamuddin Ahmad, The Wahabi Movement in India (Calcutta, Firma K.L. Mukhopadhyah, 1966), p. 37. See also Mohiuddin Ahmad, Saiyid Ahmad Shahid (Lucknow, Academy of Islamic Research and Publications, 1975).

[17] M. Saghir Hasan Ma'sumi, trans., Imam Razi's 'Ilm al-Akhlaq (Islamabad, Pakistan, Islamic Research Institute, 1969), p. 55, no. 4, quoting M. Abdul Haqq Ansari, The Ethical Philosophy of Miskawaih, Aligarh, 1965.

[18] Syed Ahmad Khan Bahadur, A Series of Essays on the Life of Muhammad and subjects subsidiary thereto (Lahore, Premier Book House, reprinted 1968), p. xv.

[19] Ibid., pp. 351, 352.

[20] L. Troll, Sayyid Ahmad Khan, pp. 235, 236.

[21] For a comparison of medieval and modern views of jihad, see R. Peters, Jihad in Medieval and Modern Islam (Leiden, Brill, 1977).

[22] Syed Ahmad Khan Bahadur, Review on Dr. Hunter's Indian Musalmans Are They Bound in Conscience to Rebel against the Queen? (Lahore, Premier Book House, n.d.).

[23] Shan Mohammad, ed., Writings, p. 254.

[24] Graham, The Life and Work of Sir Syed Ahmed Khan, p. 101.

[25] Dar, Religious Thought, p. 250.

[26] Ibid., pp. 239-66.

[27] Ibid., pp. 156, 157.

[28] Syed Ahmad Khan Bahadur, A Series of Essays, pp. 162-64.

[29] Ibid., p. 342.

[30] Ibid., pp. 207, 208.

[31] Muhammad Abdullah Khan Khushgi, ed., Maqalat-i-Sir Syed, pp. 60-65. See also M.M. Siddiqui, Social Thought of Sir Syed Ahmad Khan (Osmania University, India, Da'raulu' Ma'arif Press, 1961), p. 57.

[32] Fazlur Rahman, Major Themes of the Qur'an, pp. 28, 29.

[33] Graham, The Life and Work of Sir Syed Ahmed Khan, p. 213.

[34] Muhammad Abdullah Khan Khushgi, ed., Maqalat-i-Sir Syed, pp. 201-04.

[35]Ibid., p. 205.

[36]Syed Ahmed Khan Bahadur, A Series of Essays, p. 175.

[37]Dar, Religious Thought, pp. 122, 123.

[38]Siddiqui, Social Thought, p. 117.

[39]Dar, Religious Thought, pp. 264-66.

[40]Ibid., pp. 262, 263.

[41]Shan Mohammed, ed., Writings, pp. 200, 201.

[42]Ibid., p. 183.

[43]Siddiqui, Social Thought, pp. 50-55, quoting The Journal of the Scientific Society (Aligarh, 1871), p. 14.

[44]Nizami, Sayyid Ahmad Khan, p. 151.

[45]Ibid., p. 155.

[46]Ibid., p. 159.

Notes to Chapter 3:

[1]Kalim Bahadur, The Jama'at-i-Islami of Pakistan (New Delhi, Chetana Publications, 1977), pp. 13, 14. Two other sources in English about Mawdudi's life are Charles J. Adams, "The Ideology of Mawlana Mawdudi," in Donald Smith, ed., South Asian Politics and Religion (Princeton, Princeton University Press, 1966) and Khurshid Ahmad and Zafar Ishfaq Ansari, ed., Islamic Perspectives, Studies in Honour of Mawlana Sayyid Abu A'la Mawdudi (Jeddah, Saudi Publishing House, 1979).

[2]For information about the Muslim Brotherhood, see Richard Mitchell, The Society of the Muslim Brothers (London, Oxford University Press, 1969).

[3]Kalim Bahadur, The Jama'at-i-Islami, p. 145.

[4]Sayyid Abul Ala Mawdudi, The Ethical Viewpoint of Islam (Lahore, Markazi Maktaba Jama'at-i-Islam, 1947), pp. 1-8.

[5]Ibid., pp. 8-29.

[6]Ibid., pp. 29-30.

[7]Ibid., pp. 33-35.

[8]Misbahul Islam Faruqi, Introducing Mawdudi (Karachi, Student Publications Bureau, 1968), p. 7.

[9]Ibid., p. 4.

[10]Abul Ala Maudoodi, "Economic and Political Teachings of the Qur'an," in M.M. Sharif, ed., A History of Muslim Philosophy, vol. 1 (Wiesbaden, Otto Harrassowitz, 1963), pp. 181, 182.

[11]Ibid., p. 190.

[12]Ibid., p. 185.

[13]Ibid., p. 193.

[14]Ibid., p. 197.

[15]Sayyid Abul Ala Maudoodi, The Process of Islamic Revolution (Lahore, Maktaba Jama'at-e-Islami, 2nd edition, 1955), p. 58.

[16]Abul Ala Maududi, The Meaning of the Qur'an, vol. 5 (Lahore, Islamic Publications, Ltd., 1971), p. 165.

[17]Sayyid Abul Ala Mawdudi, A Short History of the Revivalist Movement in Islam, trans. by al-Ashari (Lahore, Islamic Publications, seventh edition, reprinted 1963), p. iii.

[18]Cheich si Boubakeur Hamza, Le Coran, traduction nouvelle et commentaires, 2 vols. (Paris, fayard/denoel, 1972).

[19]Abul Ala Maudidi, The Meaning of the Qur'an, vol. 4, p. 124.

[20]Ibid., p. 205.

[21]For a discussion of the religious function of paradigm, see Ian Barbour, Myth, Models and Paradigms (London, SCM Press, 1974).

[22]Abul Ala Maududi, The Meaning of the Qur'an, vol. 5, p. 121.

[23]Sharif, ed., A History of Muslim Philosophy, vol. 1, p. 198.

[24]Sharif, ed., A History of Muslim Philosophy, p. 195.

[25]Kalim Bahadur, The Jama'at-i-Islami, pp. 105-112.

[26]Charles J. Adams, "The Ideology of Mawlana Mawdudi," in Donald E. Smith, ed., South Asian Politics and Religion, p. 389.

[27]For a discussion of the inter-action between Mawdudi and the ulama see Leonard Binder, Religion and Politics in Pakistan (Berkeley, University of California Press).

[28]Abul Ala Maududi, Purdah and the Status of Woman in Islam, trans. by al-Ashari (Lahore, Islamic Publications, 1972, p. iii.

[29]Abul Ala Maududi, The Meaning of the Qur'an, vol. 4, p. 16.

[30]Abul Ala Maududi, Purdah and the Status of Woman in Islam, p. 83.

[31]Ibid., p. 91.

[32]Ibid., p. 166.

[33]Ibid., pp. 136-138.

[34]Ibid., p. 173.

[35]Ibid., p. 173.

[36]Abul Ala Maududi, The Meaning of the Qur'an, vol. 2, p. 309.

[37]Ibid., p. 318.

[38]Norman Anderson, Law Reform in the Muslim World (London, The Athlone Press, 1976), p. 100.

Notes to Chapter 4:

[1]Peter Berger, The Heretical Imperative: Contemporary Possibilities of Religious Affirmation (New York, Anchor Books, 1980), pp. 20, 21.

[2]Ibid., pp. 56-60.

[3]Muhammad Iqbal, The Reconstruction of Religious Thought in Islam, pp. 14, 15, 167.

[4]Muhammad Ali, My Life a Fragment (Lahore, Ashraf, 1942), p. 88.

[5]Iqbal, The Reconstruction of Religious Thought in Islam, p. 167.

[6]Muhammad Mujeeb, The Indian Muslims (Montreal, McGill University Press, 1971).

[7]Ziya-al-Hasan Faruqi, The Deoband School and the Demand for Pakistan (Bombay, Asia Publishing House, 1963).

[8]Muhammad Abdullah Khan Khushgi, ed., Maqalat-i-Sir-Syed, p. 50.

[9]Hafeez Malik and Morris Dembo, trans., Sir Sayyid Ahmed Khan's History of the Bijnore Rebellion, p. 104.

[10]Afzal Iqbal, The Prophet's Diplomacy (Cape Cod, Mass., Claude, Stark & Co., 1975).

[11]M.M. Sharif, ed., A History of the Muslim Philosophy, vol. 1, p. 229. See also George Hourani, "Reason and Revelation in Ibn Hazm's Ethical Thought" in Parwiz Morewedge, ed., Islamic Philosophical Theology (Albany, State University of New York Press, 1979).

[12]James Barr, Fundamentalism (Philadelphia, The Westminister Press, 1977), p. 2.

[13]Noah Brannen, Sok Gakkai Japan's Militant Buddhists (John Knox Press, 1968).

[14]Kalim Bahadur, The Jama'at-i-Islami, pp. 129-135.

[15]Iris Murdoch, The Sovereignty of Good (London, Routledge & Kegan Paul, 1970), pp. 1, 40.

[16]Iris Murdoch, The Fire and the Sun, Why Plato Banished the Artists (London, Oxford University Press, 1972), p. 57.

[17]P. Hardy, The Muslims of British India (Cambridge, Cambridge University Press, 1972), p. 61.

[18]Muhammad Abdullah Khan Khushgi, ed., Maqalat-i-Sir Syed, p. 99.

[19]Ziya-al-Hasan Faruqi, The Deoband School and the Demand for Pakistan.

[20]Siddiqui, Social Thought of Sir Sayyid Ahmed Khan, pp. 48-51.

[21]Coulson, A history of Islamic Law, pp. 77, 78.

[22]William James, The Varieties of Religious Experience (New York, The Modern Library, 1936).

[23]D. Lelyveld, Aligarh's First Generation, Muslim Solidarity in British India (Princeton, Princeton University Press, 1978).

[24]C. Zurayk, The Refinement of Character, pp. 25, 26.

[25]Tom Driver, Christ in a Changing World: Towards an Ethical Christology (New York, Crossroads, 1981), p. 22.

[26]Iqbal, The Reconstruction of Religious Thought in Islam, p. 180.

[27]Berger, The Heretical Imperative, pp. 72-80. For another recent philosophical discussion of the need to recover a sense of civilised life see Alasdair MacIntyre After Virtue (University of Notre Dame Press, 1981).

[28]See Berger, The Heretical Imperative, Chapter 3, n. 35.

Index

SR SUPPLEMENTS

EDITIONS SR

2. **THE CONCEPTION OF PUNISHMENT IN EARLY INDIAN LITERATURE**
   Terence P. Day
   1982 / iv + 328 pp.

3. **TRADITIONS IN CONTACT AND CHANGE**
   Selected Proceedings of the XIVth Congress of the International Association for the History of Religions
   Edited by Peter Slater and Donald Wiebe with Maurice Boutin and Harold Coward
   1983 / x + 758 pp.

4. **LE MESSIANISME DE LOUIS RIEL**
   Gilles Martel
   1984 / xviii + 484 p.

5. **MYTHOLOGIES AND PHILOSOPHIES OF SALVATION IN THE THEISTIC TRADITIONS OF INDIA**
   Klaus K. Klostermaier
   1984 / xvi + 552 pp.

6. **AVERROES' DOCTRINE OF IMMORTALITY**
   A Matter of Controversy
   Ovey N. Mohammed
   1984 / vi + 202 pp.

STUDIES IN CHRISTIANITY AND JUDAISM / ETUDES SUR LE CHRISTIANISME ET LE JUDAISME

1. **A STUDY IN ANTI-GNOSTIC POLEMICS**
   Irenaeus, Hippolytus, and Epiphanius
   Gérard Vallée
   1981 / xii + 114 pp.

THE STUDY OF RELIGION IN CANADA / SCIENCES RELIGIEUSES AU CANADA

1. **RELIGIOUS STUDIES IN ALBERTA**
   A State-of-the-Art Review
   Ronald W. Neufeldt
   1983 / xiv + 145 pp.

COMPARATIVE ETHICS

1. **MUSLIM ETHICS AND MODERNITY**
   A Comparative Study of the Ethical Thought of Sayyid Ahmad Khan and Mawlana Mawdudi
   Sheila McDonough
   1984 / x + 130 pp.

Also published / Avons aussi publié
RELIGION AND CULTURE IN CANADA / RELIGION ET CULTURE AU CANADA
Edited by / sous la direction de
Peter Slater
1977 / viii + 568 pp. / OUT OF PRINT

Available from / en vente chez:

Wilfrid Laurier University Press
Wilfrid Laurier University
Waterloo, Ontario, Canada   N2L 3C5

Published for the
Canadian Corporation for Studies in Religion/
Corporation Canadienne des Sciences Religieuses
by Wilfrid Laurier University Press